Tucson
a
Basketball Town

Bob Elliott and Eric Money

Tucson a Basketball Town

Published by Wheatmark*
1760 East River Road, Suite 145
Tucson, Arizona 85718
U.S.A.
www.wheatmark.com

ISBN: 978-1-62787-041-2 (paperback)
ISBN: 978-1-62787-042-9 (ebook)

LCCN: 2014931111

TABLE OF CONTENTS

TABLE OF CONTENTS

FOREWORD

As an eighteen-year-old black student-athlete from Ann Arbor, Michigan, the journey to Tucson, Arizona, started as an opportunity to attend and play basketball for one of the greatest collegiate institutions in America: the University of Arizona. In the early 1970s, I, like others, experienced race riots, a movement to accept and be proud of your black heritage, and enjoyed the music out of Motown. I had the opportunity to experience a top-notch sports program and educational institution that helped shape me into the person I am today. Thankfully, it was all given in stewardship from the Tucson community support that has grown this village into a true college basketball town.

I made the choice to come to the UA to be a part of history under Coach Fred Snowden, the first African American head basketball coach at a major university in a major conference. At that time in history, no black coach had ever made it to the NCAA tournament, let alone had won it.

Coach Snowden came to Tucson and created an environment where opponents were fearful to play the UA in McKale Center. Lute Olson (head coach from 1983 to 2007) extended this tradition, including the amazing 1997 national championship team. Sean Miller (head coach from 2009 to the present) will add his own asphalt to that road of success.

But there is only one first, and in this book you will be able to understand how Tucson became a basketball town beginning with the arrival of Coach Snowden in 1972.

Fred "the Fox" Snowden was a trailblazer in his own right, but his role as the coach who initiated the spirit of basketball in Tucson is often overlooked. Now Coach Snowden can be held in the proper esteem for being the first black head coach in the NCAA Division I in a major conference, as well as the first University of Arizona coach to take his team to the Elite Eight of the NCAA tournament. Coach Snowden should be commended for developing and establishing Tucson as the wonderful basketball town that we enjoy.

Bob "Big Bird" Elliott
University of Arizona Basketball 1973–1977
BS Business Administration 1977
MBA Eller College 1984

CHAPTER 1

ARIZONA BASKETBALL BEFORE 1972

The University of Arizona began its intercollegiate basketball program in 1904. Between 1904 and 1914, there were five head coaches. During this period, the coach with the longest tenure (1906 to 1911) is simply listed in the *Arizona Basketball Press Guide* as "unknown."

In 1914, J. F. "Pop" McKale took over for Ray Quigley, and the dynasty began. Pop McKale coached the Wildcats from 1914 to 1921, compiling a 49–12 record with three undefeated seasons while also coaching football and baseball. He held the position of director of athletics for forty-three years, setting a tone of continuity and longevity that would become the trademark of all Arizona sports programs. When Pop McKale decided that he was spread too thin, he divested himself of responsibilities, and the basketball program was handed off to a series of short-term placeholders. James Pierce held a great 27–5 record in his two seasons. He was replaced by Basil Stanley

(1923–24) and Walter Davis (1924–25) who each held the position for one year.

In 1925 Pop McKale hired Fred A. Enke to take over for Walter Davis. During that first year for Fred Enke the basketball team lost more games than it won (their final record was 6–7). Arizona would not have a losing record after Enke's first season until the 1941–42 season.

There were bright spots and accomplished student athletes in Arizona basketball during Enke's coaching years. For example, Mo Udall, the tall, lanky kid from the little Arizona town of St. Johns, was the Wildcat captain in 1948 and an all-conference member of a 19–10 team. He was even drafted by the Denver Nuggets of the National Basketball League (NBL). Mo went on to earn a law degree from the University of Arizona and served as a member of the United States House of Representatives for the state of Arizona from 1961 to 1991.

Coach Enke proceeded to win twelve Border Conference championships and had the Cats in the national rankings during the 1950s. He won 60 percent of his games over thirty-six seasons. He took the Cats to the National Invitational

Tournament (NIT) in 1950 and 1951, and he then took them to the National Collegiate Athletic Association (NCAA) tournament in 1951. Roger Johnson, who played from 1948 to 1952, was the first All-American at Arizona. Bruce Larson, the only person to both play for (1948–1950) and be a head coach for Arizona (1961–1972), said, "Roger could run and shoot. He could have played with the players of today."

The history of Arizona is rich in politics, frontier, military stations, border protections, and battles that helped shape the southwestern region of the United States. Although Arizona is not widely associated with the Civil War, the Mexican-American War, or the War of 1812, Arizona was considered a southern state despite its western location. The westernmost battle of the Civil War was fought just up Interstate 10 at a desolate outpost known today as Picacho Peak.

Tucson was pragmatic and too poor to have total segregation, so it settled for planting the seeds of second-class citizenship into its colored population. Tucson segregated its elementary and junior high schools until 1951. Because the community had only two high schools, students were integrated once they reached the ninth grade. The city's leaders thought that by that age, everyone would understand their places in society and would not transgress from them.

Tucson took on issues of segregation in a unique manner. For example, it had no slums in the traditional sense. People with more money lived in one area of town, and those with less lived elsewhere. Some of the Hispanic citizens of Tucson lived in the Barrio Historico, Barrio Anita, and Barrio Tiburon near the community's sewer system. Many blacks and whites harvested the cotton fields of nearby Marana. In Tucson, segregation's power was more often a product of means and entitlement than of skin color.

Coach Enke was the man at the helm when Arizona introduced its first black basketball player, three-sport superstar Hadie Redd, in 1954. Redd struggled against segregation. He was not allowed to stay in hotels in some towns and was forced to sleep in local homes, "colored" boarding houses, or even the gym itself. Arizona was in the Border Conference during those years, and the schools (Hardin-Simmons, New Mexico, New Mexico State, UTEP, Texas Tech, West Texas State, Northern

Arizona, and Arizona State), were located in the states of Arizona, New Mexico, and Texas.

From 1957 to 1960, Ernie McCray was the Cats' best player and leading scorer. His single game scoring record of 46 points still stands as the symbol of excellence in the Arizona basketball program. He was also the first Arizona basketball player to average a double-double in his career at 17.8 points per game and 10.8 rebounds per game. Joe Skaisgir (1961–1962) was the second of three in the history of Arizona basketball players to average a double-double in his career at 19.9 points per game and 11.2 rebounds per game. When Coach Enke retired in 1961, he was the all-time winningest coach in UA basketball history.

John Wooden at UCLA was causing some mild consternation out West. With all-everything players like Walt Hazzard, Wooden had broken through to win the NCAA national titles in 1964 and 1965. It was the beginning of an NCAA championship run that had never been seen before and would not be seen again. Each team was headlined by a black All-American player, except for the 1965 team, which was led by the white, left-handed, sharp-shooting Gail Goodrich.

At that time in the 1960s college programs commonly (and quietly) agreed that you could have two and even three black players in the starting lineup. You could also put four on the floor if the game was in doubt and you needed to win. In the West and the South, this "gentlemen's agreement" was still quietly enforced. There were a few black players in the Southeastern Conference (SEC), but there were more than enough historically black colleges and universities like Grambling, Morgan State, and Howard, where young black men could excel in academics and athletics and have a social collegiate experience. Even with some progress toward equality many predominately white colleges and universities did not have black student-athletes to matriculate at their school.

In 1966 the Texas Western Miners, now known as the University of Texas at El Paso (UTEP), became the first school to win the NCAA championship with a starting lineup of five black players. Texas Western coach Don Haskins turned his nose on the "gentlemen's agreement," by starting five black players, and he succeeded by winning the NCAA tournament. What made the event newsworthy was that the Miners defeated legendary Kentucky coach Adolph Rupp and his all-white team of Wildcats in the championship game. The Kentucky Wildcats, led by Pat Riley and Lou Dampier, were affectionately known as "Rupp's Runts." The national media had headlined the game as black versus white. The world of basketball had never commanded such hype. This legendary story was eventually turned into the movie, *Glory Road*. This wasn't a Jackie Robinson story or the story of a lone warrior against the status quo to change things for all time. Black men were finally given an equal opportunity to play basketball at the collegiate level with their white counterparts.

That year the Miners played Coach Bruce Larson's Arizona Wildcats in El Paso on February 10, 1966, and Texas Western escaped with a nine-point victory in overtime (81–72). Coach Larson said, "We could have won that game in regulation. The game was tied, and we took the last shot in regulation, and it went in and out." Arizona's record that year was 15–11. Ted Pickett led the Cats in scoring, and Mike Aboud led them in rebounding.

In February 1972, BYU came to town to play the Wildcats. During this time in US history, race relations were being challenged. A boycott was called by the University of Arizona black students against BYU because of their religious beliefs. Larson said, "The game was delayed, and the police were very visible. We had five black players, and I knew they [the black players] wanted to do something, but we did not know what that would be. Eventually the game was played without an incident."

CHAPTER 2

THE HIRING OF
FRED SNOWDEN

To describe John Schaefer in a word today would be to say he had swag. "Swag" is what the kids say when something is hip or cool. In 1971 John Schaefer was cool. He wore his hair longer than most men of his stature, and he wore sideburns. His tie knots were large, and he wore a wide lapel and slightly mod jackets and suits. His looks belied his pedigree: an undergraduate degree from the Polytechnic Institute of Brooklyn and a doctorate from the University of Illinois. When he headed west to take a job teaching chemistry at the University of California, Berkeley, he had no idea that he would never live on the East Coast again.

Two years later he was hired to teach chemistry at the UA. When he became the fifteenth president of the University of Arizona, he was thirty-six years old, and he would make his mark in history. Reaching the pinnacle of your career at thirty-six years old could leave a man with too much time and no worlds left to conquer, but not for John

Schaefer. For one thing, Tucson was the type of city that would intrigue him. He traveled all over the Southwest on his Harley and flew around the world. From that time on, he knew Tucson would be the place for him and his wife, Helen, to raise their two daughters—a place to return to. Only a progressive institution anxious to be seen as big time would have the gravas to hire a man his age with his obviously progressive stance and ideas. After all, his predecessor, Richard Harville, had retired after nearly forty years of service with the University of Arizona and had been the president for two decades. Times were changing. Schaefer's Arizona was preparing to wade into deeper waters, and there would be no turning back.

Schaefer liked sports in general and basketball about as much as anyone. "But I don't know what possessed President Harville, my predecessor, to build a fourteen thousand-seat arena with the kind of unsuccessful basketball program we had and to expect to fill it," he said.

Schaefer had to hire a new athletic director, as Dick Clausen had announced his retirement. He called his colleague at the University of Michigan, Dr. Robben Fleming, for counsel. The Big Ten

Conference was probably the dominant college conference in the nation on the strength of its football programs and with the state of Michigan having a stranglehold on the country's auto manufacturing and agricultural base.

President Fleming suggested President Schaefer meet the current associate athletic director at the University of Michigan, Dave Strack. Strack was very well known in college basketball, as he was the former head basketball coach of Michigan in 1965 when the Wolverines beat Bill Bradley's Princeton team in the semifinal game, only to lose to Coach John Wooden and the UCLA Bruins 91–80 in the NCAA championship that year. Strack was hired as the athletic director by the University of Arizona in the spring of 1972.

This would be the last year that Larson would be the head basketball coach at Arizona. Strack and Schaefer decided that a change was needed for the Arizona basketball program. There were some people who thought Bruce Larson deserved an opportunity to open McKale Center and continue as the head coach. "That wasn't going to happen just because the man was a nice guy," recalled Strack.

Dr. Schaefer and Strack discussed Schaefer's

desire to have a good athletic program. President Schaefer stated, "It was time for black coaches in basketball. I really did believe that. It was just ridiculous to look at the NCAA tournament or the NIT. The game was being dominated by black players, and yet you didn't have a single black coach in the country." There was a shrewd angle to the thinking of Dr. Schaefer. "I thought it would be good for Arizona. We had a pretty marginal basketball program for the past decade or so, and a black coach would probably have a leg up on recruiting good black players."

There were tons of young, hungry assistants looking for a place—and a chance—to make their mark as a head coach. George Raveling was the promising young black assistant coach with the University of Maryland, known as "the UCLA of the East," as Maryland Head Coach Charles "Lefty" Driesell liked to put it. Raveling was hired later that year in 1972 as the head coach at Washington State University of the then Pac-8 Conference. Denny Crum was an understudy to Coach Wooden at UCLA, before the University of Louisville eventually hired Crum in 1971 as its head basketball coach. In 1980 Coach Crum took Louisville to a NCAA national title. John Thompson was a very successful black head coach at St. Anthony's High School in Washington, DC, before moving on to be the head coach with the Georgetown Hoyas in 1972. In 1984 Coach Thompson would become the first black head coach to win a NCAA championship. There was a very promising young head coach at Cal Long Beach named Lute Olson (who later took Arizona to its one and only NCAA championship in 1997) who replaced the legendary Jerry "Tark the Shark" Tarkanian in 1973 when Tark had moved on to build a national power at the University of Nevada at Las Vegas. Mike Krzyzewski (who would later lead Duke University to multiple NCAA championships in 1991, 1992, 2001, and 2010) mentored under Head Coach Bob Knight for the 1974–75 season at Indiana University.

But Strack didn't have anyone else in mind other than Fred Snowden. "He just ran such a disciplined program in what was a tough part of Detroit, and I thought, boy, if he can handle it there, he can handle it anywhere. He was my one and only choice," Strack said. "I remember Fred coached at Northwestern High School, and he ran a very tight ship. You didn't curse; you didn't swear. In the gym, if you got out of line, Freddy would just point, and you were out of the gym, and there was no recourse."

When Snowden was hired as an assistant at Michigan, Strack was the associate athletic director to the visionary athletic director Don Canham, and Johnny Orr was the head men's basketball coach. Strack remembered that even though Snowden hated to fly, he got on a plane and came out, even if it took a few drinks before he would get on a plane. In the Big Ten he would often leave Ann Arbor early and drive to the road games, rather than fly with the team because of his fear of flying.

Strack recommended Fred Snowden for the head coach position. He hired Snowden twice, first as the assistant coach at Michigan and then as the head coach at the UA. Schaefer and Strack made history as they hired Fred Snowden as the first black head basketball coach at a major university in a major conference!

Dr. Schaefer and Strack's vision of having a good athletic program was starting to materialize. "I hired (basketball coach) Fred (Snowden) in 1972 and (football coach) Jim Young in 1973. That was a good pair," Strack said.

UNIVERSITY OF ARIZONA

———————— Tucson, Arizona 85721 ————————

SPORTS INFORMATION

Frank W. Soltys *Director*   AREA CODE 602, 884-1919

Fred Snowden, assistant basketball coach at the University of Michigan for the past four years, has been named head basketball coach at the University of Arizona it was announced today by UofA Athletic Director Dave Strack.

Snowden, 35, (born April 3, 1936), succeeds Bruce Larson who resigned at the conclusion of this past season.

In announcing the appointment Strack said, "we feel that we have selected in Fred Snowden an outstanding young man who has a great knowledge of basketball and possesses the qualities to become a very successful collegiate head coach. I have known Fred personally for 10 years. He is a gentleman, a fine family man and is very well respected by his peers in the coaching profession."

A Detroit native, Snowden attended Northwestern High where he was outstanding in both basketball and baseball. Following graduation he enrolled at Wayne State where he was team captain in his senior year in both sports. He was a 5-9 guard in basketball and a shortstop in baseball and won all-conference honors in both sports.

Following graduation (BS, 1958) he returned to his high school alma mater and in four four years (1958-62) as a junior varsity coach his teams posted a phenomenal record of 80-0. He moved up to the varsity for the next six years (1963-1968) and had almost equal success posting a 101-7 record, and winning five straight Detroit city championship championships. He also coached varsity baseball from 1963 through 1968 and posted a 31-14 record. He was awarded his Master's degree from Wayne State in 1965.

In 1968, when Dave Strack gave up varsity coaching at Michigan, Snowden became the assistant coach to the new Michigan coach Johnny Orr. He has served in that capacity since.

Snowden is married (wife Mae) and has two children, Charles 18, and Stacey 8.

1,1A,2,2A   -30-

Coach Fred Snowden Arizona Press Release (page 1)

PROFESSIONAL STARS WHO PREPPED UNDER SNOWDEN:

Willie Horton   - Detroit Tigers

Alex Johnson   - Cleveland Indians

John Mayberry   - Kansas City Royals

Ron Johnson   - New York Football Giants

Matt Snorton   - Denver Football Broncos - A.F.L.

Henry Carr   - Olympic Gold Medal Track Winner and
                    New York Football Giants

Rich Coggins   - Baltimore Oriole Organization

Lincoln Clark   - Montreal Expos Organization

COLLEGIATE BASKETBALL PLAYERS WHO PREPPED UNDER SNOWDEN:

Roland Stamps   - University of Arizona - 1967

Stand Washington   - Michigan State University - All American - 1966

Ben McGilmer   - University of Iowa - Co-Captain - 1969-70

Jim Pitts   - University of Michigan - All Big Ten - 1967-68

Richard Carter   - University of Michigan - 1968

Curtis Lloyd   - Pepperdine College, California - 1967

Lamont King   - Long Beach State University - 1972

PLAYERS RECRUITED WHILE ASSISTANT COACH AT UNIVERSITY OF MICHIGAN:

	Home State
Henry Wilmore - All American - 1970-72	New York
Ken Brady - All Big Ten - 3rd Team - 1970-71	Michigan
John Kantner - High School All American - 1971	Ohio
Campy Russell - High School All American 1st Team Captain '71	Michigan
Doug Ashworth - High School All American - 1971	Ohio
Joe Johnson - High School All American - 1971	Michigan

Coach Fred Snowden Arizona Press Release (page 2)

FREDRICK SNOWDEN

PERSONAL:

Born: Brewton, Alabama - April 3, 1936

Married: Mae Boga Snowden

Children: Charles Anthony Snowden - Age 19
           Stacey Rene Snowden   - Age 9

EDUCATION:

Nortwestern High School - 1954

Wayne State University - B.S. 1958 Major: Physical Education

Wayne State University - M.ED. 1965 Major: Physical Education

PROFESSIONAL EXPERIENCE:

Teacher of Health & Physical Education - McGraw Elementary
                                         Detroit, Mich. 9/58-11/58

Teacher of Health & Physical Education - Northwestern High School
                                         Detroit, Mich. 11/58-8/68

Associate Professor of Health & Physical Education - University of
                                         Michigan - 1968-1971

HIGH SCHOOL COACHING EXPERIENCE:

Junior Varsity Basketball - 1958 - 1962

Cross Country   - 1958 - 1962

Varsity Baseball   - 1963 - 1968

Varsity Basketball   - 1963 - 1968

HIGH SCHOOL COACHING RECORD:

Junior Varsity Basketball - 1958 - 1962 Won 80 Lost 0

Varsity Basketball   - 1963 - 1968 Won 87 Lost 8

Varsity Baseball   - 1963 - 1968 Won 31 Lost 14

Fred Snowden 1972 resume (page 1 of 4)

COLLEGE COACHING EXPERIENCE:

Assistant Varsity Basketball Coach - University of Michigan
                                               1968 - 1972

Head Basketball Coach   - University of Arizona
                                            March 22, 1972
                                            Record - 1st Year - Won 16 Lost 10

AWARDS:

1972-73 NCAA District 7 - Coach of the Year

1972-73 Western Athletic Conference Coach of the Year

1972   Appointed by President Richard Nixon to the Environmental
        Merit Awards Commission

PROFESSIONAL ACTIVITIES:

President Elect - Detroit Scholastic Coaches Association

Member   - Michigan High School Coaches Association

Member   - Varsity Club of Detroit Incorporated

Member   - Michigan Federation of Teachers

Member   - Detroit Federation of Teachers

Member   - The National Association of Basketball Coaches
               of the United States

COMMUNITY ACTIVITIES:

Participant   - Northwestern High School Parent-Teacher-
               Student Association

Participant   - Northwestern High School Alumnae
               Association Incorporated

Participant   - Northwestern High School Men's Club Inc.

Participant   - Outer Drive Faith Lutheran Church Youth
               Activity Program Organization

Co-Director   - Ann Arbor Michigan Free Summer Basketball
               Clinic and Lectures

Fred Snowden 1972 resume (page 2 of 4)

MEDIA EXPERIENCE:

1968-1971 - "Coaches Comment" - Post Basketball Game Radio
            Interview Show - Station WAAM, Ann Arbor

1968-1971 - Television Interviews with numerous Sportscasters on
            various TV Stations throughout the country in position
            as Assistant Basketball Coach at University of Michigan.

1971-1972 - Sports Telecaster - W. J. B. K. TV 2, Southfield, Michigan

1972   - Radio Play by Play Broadcast of N.A.A.C.P. Black Charities
            Football Game - W.G.P.R., Detroit, Michigan

1972-1973 - The Fred Snowden show in present position as Head
            Basketball Coach at the University of Arizona for KGUN-TV
            Channel 9.

PROFESSIONAL BASEBALL BACKGROUND:

1962-1967 - Territorial Baseball Scout for Milwaukee Braves and
            Atlanta Braves for Michigan, Ohio, Indiana and Windsor area.

PROFESSIONAL STARS WHO PREPPED UNDER SNOWDEN:

Willie Horton   - Detroit Tigers

Alex Johnson   - Cleveland Indians

John Mayberry   - Kansas City Royals

Ron Johnson   - New York Football Giants

Matt Snorton   - Denver Football Broncos - A.F.L.

Henry Carr   - Olympic Gold Medal Track Winner and
                    New York Football Giants

Rich Coggins   - Baltimore Oriole Organization

Lincoln Clark   - Montreal Expos Organization

Henry Reed   - New York Football Giants

Fred Snowden 1972 resume (page 3 of 4)

COLLEGIATE BASKETBALL PLAYERS WHO PREPPED UNDER SNOWDEN:

Roland Stamps	- University of Arizona - 1967
Stan Washington	- Michigan State University All American - 1966
Ben McGilmer	- University of Iowa - Co-Captain - 1969-70
Jim Pitts	- University of Michigan - All Big Ten - 1967-68
Richard Carter	- University of Michigan - 1968
Curtis Lloyd	- Pepperdine College, California - 1967
Lamont King	- Long Beach State University - 1972

PLAYERS RECRUITED WHILE ASSISTANT COACH AT UNIVERSITY OF MICHIGAN

		Home State
Henry Wilmore	- All American - 1970-71	New York
Ken Brady	- All Big Ten - 3rd Team - 1970-71	Michigan
John Kantner	- High School All American - 1971	Ohio
Campy Russell	- High School All American 1st Team Captain - 1971	Michigan
Doug Ashworth	- High School All American - 1971	Ohio
Joe Johnson	- High School All American - 1971	Michigan

Fred Snowden 1972 resume (page 4 of 4)

CHAPTER 3

THE FIRST SEASON
1972–1973
Tucson Becomes a Basketball Town

B efore you can get players, you have to get a staff. Jerry Holmes was looking for a job—any job. Holmes had worked in the past as an assistant baseball and assistant basketball coach in Pennsylvania. Holmes said, "I decided it was time for me to get a job, a four-year job, so I packed up and went to LA to attend the Final Four."

Holmes ran into John McClendon, who at that time was a Converse representative but was better known as the great basketball coach at the historically black Tennessee State University. McClendon led Holmes to Fred Snowden, who had just been named head basketball coach at the University of Arizona. McClendon called Coach Snowden and arranged an interview between Snowden and Holmes.

Holmes remembers, "That was the first time I ever saw the product Magic Shave. I go knock on his hotel room. He's in there shaving. He has a

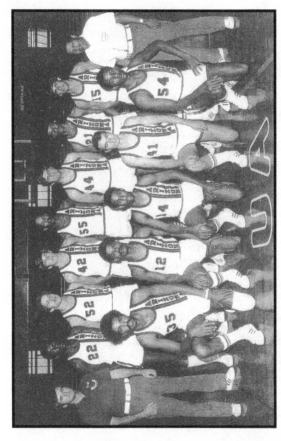

1972–1973 Arizona Basketball Team. Left to right front row: Lynard Harris, Ron Allen, Eric Money, Tom Lawson, Al Fleming. Left to right, back row: Assistant Coach Jerry Holmes, Coniel Norman, Jim Wakefield, Paul Strong, John Irving, Phil Edwards, Randy Echols, Jim Rappis, Coach Fred Snowden butter knife out and he says I've got thirty minutes because he was meeting his brother for dinner tonight. That was about six forty-five. I left that room at eleven thirty."

Snowden hired Holmes. "I was scared," Holmes admitted. "[I thought] This is the first black coach in a major conference, and I want him to be successful. It meant a lot to me to be the first assistant of the first black coach to take over a major college program." Holmes went to see his old coach and mentor from Scranton Prep High School, Black-Jack Gallagher, who told him, "The best thing an assistant coach can do for a head coach is to be loyal."

Now with a lead assistant coach, Snowden and Holmes could recruit talented players because you can forget having great success as a team at the Division One level of NCAA basketball without talent.

Coach Snowden was an advocate for student-athletes receiving their degrees. He had both a bachelor's and a master's degree. Coach Snowden stressed education. You would always see Coach Snowden reading newspapers to keep abreast of current events. Snowden's combination of education and basketball knowledge would be attractive to a recruit and his parents.

This 1972–1973 basketball season would be the first year the NCAA would allow freshman student-athletes to play on a varsity team. This was one major game changer in the history of college athletics.

"Don't worry, Coach," Snowden told Strack. "I already got the franchise." The "franchise" was a sixteen-year-old six foot, one inch guard from Kettering High School in inner-city Detroit named Eric Money. Money and his talents fit in with the WAC Conference. "The WAC was a run and gun conference. UTEP was going to hold the ball if you let them, but Utah, New Mexico, with Michael Cooper and that bunch, played an upbeat style of basketball. Utah had Ticky Burden and Mike Sojourner, and BYU and ASU would all run," remembered Money.

With Coach Snowden's Detroit influence, Snowden also recruited small forward Coniel Norman, a teammate of Money's at Kettering High School.

Holmes had a beat on an athletic center by the

*Coach Fred Snowden and Assistant Coach
Jerry Holmes, 1973*

name of John Irving from Delaware who would become the starting center that year.

Next Snowden had his sights on a power forward from Michigan City, Indiana, named Al Fleming. As Snowden and Holmes did their due diligence on Fleming and his family, they found out that the name of Al's mother was Arizona Fleming. Needless to say, if you gave Fred Snowden a card like that to play, there was no way Al Fleming was not going to play basketball at the University of Arizona.

With four freshmen already recruited (a point guard, a small forward, a power forward, and a center), Snowden and Holmes set their sights on a shooting guard from Waukesha, Wisconsin. Jimmy Rappis had only two demands about where he would play college basketball. "I played an up-tempo game in high school, and so I was looking for an up-tempo program. I wanted to go someplace warm," he recalled.

Georgia and LSU were the leading contenders, with the local Jesuit school, Marquette, a long shot. Rappis remembers, "LSU Coach Dale Brown was interested, and they had just built the [Pete] Maravich Center."

When Rappis visited Georgia, he was introduced to just two black players. "We were playing, and I remember thinking, 'I'm the best player on the floor. I don't want to be the best player on the floor. I want to win.'"

Then Arizona came into the recruiting picture for Rappis. Rappis remembers his first phone conversation with Fred Snowden. "He said 'Howdy Partner, I'm Fred Snowden,' and I remember picturing Don Haskins (the head coach at UTEP) in my mind."

Assistant Coach Jerry Holmes was sent by Snowden to visit Rappis in Waukesha. Holmes told Rappis they had signed Indiana's Mr. Basketball, top recruit Al Fleming. "Once I got to Arizona [on a recruiting trip] and met the players Coach was bringing in, I was in," Rappis said.

"One night all the recruits showed up at Bear Down Gymnasium. It is a common practice on a recruiting trip for the recruit to play pickup games with the returning players so he can see where he will fit with this team both athletically and socially. The seniors were there too, guys like Tom Lawson, Lynard Harris, and Jim Wakefield. There were some competitive games." Rappis remembered leaving the gym thinking, "Let's see how many games we can win."

This was the birth of the famed Kiddie Korp squad, as Coach Fred Snowden started five freshmen. The Kiddie Korp was the number-one recruiting class that year in the nation as named by the *Street and Smith* basketball magazine.

Eric Money remembers that first year vividly and the talent the program possessed. "When you look at our team, we had three starters who went on to play in the [NBA] league my freshman year, Coniel, Al, and me. The next year we had four when Bob came in. Four out of five, that's a lot of talent. And that's not counting Germ (Herman Harris)."

Steve Kanner was a walk-on sophomore that year, one of the few holdovers from Bruce Larson's team. "One of the most memorable moments of Fred's first year was the first public scrimmage (now known as the Red/Blue game). The game went into six overtimes. Eric Money had 53 points, and Coniel Norman 38. Many others, Jim Rappis, Al Fleming, John Irving, and Ron Allen, had 20 or more. The energy in the gym was ecstatic. The uptempo action excited the crowd in Bear Down

Gym, and the competitive nature of the six over-times gave an unprecedented introduction to Fred's new program.

"The night we played the Red/Blue scrimmage was unchartered territory. We'd been practicing for a few weeks, and it was time to play in public and get ready for the season. There was tremendous excitement surrounding Coach Snowden and his Kiddie Korp. The talent level in the program took an immediate step up. That night was the first showcase; Motown had come to Tucson. That moment started a five-year relationship that shaped my adult life. It opened the opportunity for the full-ride scholarship Fred awarded me after the season and the chance to coach in the program as his graduate assistant.

"Fred brought a different style, a new approach, and had new tools to work with. Fred molded the pieces and presented a unique product. It was a special time and special season borne out of unique circumstances and Fred orchestrated a beautiful show. It played like Motown," said Kanner.

What was truly remarkable that first year was the attendance. Before Coach Snowden arrived at the UA, only hundreds of fans showed up for the games at Bear Down Gym. Students would come at halftime because they could get in for free and have their choice of seats. But now Bear Down was sold out, rockin' and rollin', full of fans and excitement. Television sets were installed around campus to show the basketball games because there were not any seats left. Townspeople would come to Bear Down without a ticket and sit outside just to hear the excitement. At midseason, without an established season ticket base, the team moved over from the 3,000-seat Bear Down Gym to the 14,000-seat McKale Center and sold that arena out as well.

Coach Snowden orchestrated the transformation, and the Tucson community fell in love with Arizona basketball. He used the same blueprint from his days at Detroit Northwestern High School by involving local business people such as lawyers, car dealers, travel agents, furniture salespeople, insurance agents, bankers, home builders, hotel owners, and more. A large part of the success of the Northwestern High School athletic teams can be traced to the Northwestern Men's Club, an association of Northwestern alumni who return to the school to mentor and

Eric Money playing against Arizona State, 1973

Coniel Norman playing against Arizona State, 1973

assist current student athletes. Members have included Willie Horton of the Detroit Tigers; Ron Johnson, captain of the University of Michigan 1967 football team; Alex Johnson, former professional baseball player; and Stan Washington, an administrator at Michigan State University. According to Richard "Bird" Carter, a class of 1968 Northwestern basketball player (who not only played for Coach Snowden at Northwestern High School but also followed Coach Snowden to the University of Michigan), the presence of the members gives a positive message to the current high school student-athletes.

Part of the orchestrated flair Snowden used was to make a grand entrance into McKale Center. Just before the game would start, everyone (players, coaches, fans and referees) would be in place to start the game except Coach Snowden. Then out of the tunnel would emerge Coach Snowden from under McKale and onto the basketball court. He would just stroll onto the court with a rolled-up game program in his right hand. As he slowly walked to his seat on the Arizona bench, Snowden would throw his right leg outward with a visible twitch on the right side of his mouth.

Schaefer remembers, "Freddy had the challenge of being a black coach in a white-dominated city with all of the traditional prejudices that you have and one big arena to fill at the same time. He was going to have to produce a basketball program that the community would accept, that was going to be exciting to watch, so the place would fill up . . . and by golly he did it. Fred was a charismatic personality, and it was definitely his personality that did it."

Coach Snowden also started the family program (which was permitted by the NCAA at that time). Players were connected with important people in the community who made the players part of their families. President Schaefer was fully supportive of the program: "It was good for the players, and it was good for the families as well. When you see the chief justice of the Supreme Court of Arizona, Stan Feldman, putting his arm around Herman Harris, a black kid from the Philadelphia area of Chester who has come out of a tough situation, it was good for both of them."

Bob Elliott remembers the family program well. "I was fortunate to be able to call a few families my Tucson family. My freshman year my

Coach Fred Snowden in action, 1973

Tucson family was the family of Leon and Phyllis Goodman. Coach Snowden was creative to try to place the student athletes with a family and a mentor for the career a player might want additional information about. Leon was a banker with First Interstate Bank. Phyllis is probably more well known than you would know. If you attend a home basketball game in McKale Center, and the University of Arizona Pep Band starts to rock and roll, on the big screen 'Dancing Phyllis' will appear from her same seats she has had since McKale Center opened. That is Phyllis Goodman, still enjoying Arizona basketball forty years later.

"My sophomore year I was placed with Byron Davis, a Farmers Insurance business owner. Because my fiancée and future wife had the same last name as Byron, he would constantly remind me that she was a Davis girl, and I had better treat her right. Byron rarely called me Bob; it was always Birdman. Around this same time I met Austin Agron at a Tucson Toros baseball game. Austin is known in southern Arizona as that crazy furniture store guy with the commercial and the tag 'neighbor that's a ganga.'

"In the spring of 1974, our brother-in-law was

one of the finalists for a position in the administration of Pima Community College. On the search
committee was Dr. Flavia Batteau Walton. Dr.
Walton invited my wife and I over to her house
to meet not only her husband, Bill, but also a few
of their running buddies in the black community.
They threw some great parties and barbeques. Bill
was a military man and they moved a lot over the
years, but Beverely and I saw them wherever they
lived (Las Vegas, San Antonio, Alabama, and lately
Washington, DC).

"Next door lived Flavia's parents, Mack and
Elgie Batteau (a UA graduate). A truly unbelievable, inspirational couple. Even after the Waltons
left Tucson, Beverely and I would still see the
Batteaus on a regular basis. The Waltons and
Batteaus reinforced the meaning of a black, educa-
tionally-based, loving family.

"Peter and Millie Economidis were actually
the family assigned to Jim Rappis, but it seemed
Beverely and I were over at their house most of the
time. This relationship was so strong with uncondi-
tional love. During the years when I was playing in
the NBA there was not a guarantee that I could be
there with Beverely during the births of Kimberlee

*Coach Fred Snowden and Arizona Sports Information
Director Frank Soltys, 1973*

and Marques. Millie was Bev's lamaze coach for both kids. Millie was the first to hold both of them. Pete taught me what I would call 'man love,' that it is okay to kiss your son or another male. To this day, not only with my sons and sons-in-law, but also those special male friends of our children, I will give them a hug and kiss. My last two years at the University of Arizona I was a member of the family of Mel and Enid Zuckerman. Mel and Enid have been great mentors and supporters. The Zuckermans have never missed a card for graduation or a birthday and have attended special events to support our family."

Regarding the family program and Wildcat basketball, Mel shared, "I was a basketball fan, and when Fred came, the excitement came." Mel remembered meeting Coach Snowden for lunch at Jack Sarver's Aztec Inn hotel and restaurant. Sarver was also involved as a Wildcat basketball supporter and a member of the family program, as Al Fleming was a part of the Sarver family. Zuckerman said, "The family program was set up to help keep the student athletes on track, keep the guys comfortable, and provide a home away from home." Zuckerman actually had two different players as family members during the Snowden Era, Bob Elliott and later Larry Demic.

Zuckerman remembers, "If Fred did not do what he did to start the excitement of Arizona basketball, Arizona could not have been able to attract a quality coach like Lute Olson. Fred really had community involvement. History develops history. The past allows a present and a future."

George Kalil of Kalil Bottling Company, also known as the "Arizona Basketball Super Fan," started traveling with the Cats in 1972 and still travels with the Arizona basketball team to this day. Kalil said, "The Arizona alumni had a trip going to Laramie, Wyoming, and Fort Collins, Colorado. The group was known as the Fort Collins Forty because there were forty people on the trip. At the first game at Colorado State University in Fort Collins, Colorado, there were no cheerleaders, no band, the place was 80 percent empty, and our seats were at the top of the facility. We lost 79–72 and headed to Laramie, Wyoming, for the game the next night against the University of Wyoming. I went looking for a drum to make some noise for the Cats. The drum cost twenty dollars, and the sticks cost six dollars. Two teachers who were

Left to right, Eric Money, bus driver (unnamed), and George Kalil at the University of Wyoming, March 3, 1973

married and on the trip with the Fort Collins Forty had artistic talents and painted both sides of the drum with Wildcat information. The game was on television back in Tucson, and when we returned, the drum was a Tucson folk hero. Arizona won the game 84–82. Soon after that the chancellor at BYU initiated a WAC Conference rule that no fan would be allowed to carry their own musical instruments to a game."

Kalil continues, "Crowds of fans would come out to Tucson International Airport to welcome the team back from being out of town. The whole bottom section of McKale Center would have all of the movers and shakers of Tucson. The Wildcat games became a big social event. At first you could tell the men were bringing their women to the game. Then it looked like the women were bringing their men to the game." McKale Center was the place to be.

Jonathan Rothschild, who would become the mayor of Tucson in 2011, was a high school senior at Canyon del Oro High School during this 1972–1973 season. When he saw Fred Snowden's brand of basketball, he said it was eye opening. "It was Fred Snowden who made Tucson into a basketball town," the mayor recalls. "Those Snowden teams of the seventies were a bridge to what was to come later under Coach Lute Olson." Snowden personally "changed the community" by the power of his personality. He changed Tucson forever and for a black man in those transitional times, "he was totally accepted" by the Tucson community.

Don and Marilyn Schroeder were Wildcat basketball supporters starting with the Bruce Larson years. The Schroeders and eleven other couples representing the Tucson business community approached Coach Larson to see if they could help the program. The group bought tickets together to sit in Bear Down Gymnasium. There were some things the group could not do for the student athletes because of NCAA regulations, but they did come up with a great parting senior gift for the players who had completed their eligibility. The group would send the player to Levy's store to get a dress sport coat. This group of supporters also started the annual basketball sports banquet to honor the accomplishments of the team and the individual players. They set up a 501(c)(3) corporation to assist and support the program. When the Arizona basketball team moved to McKale Center,

Don and Marilyn purchased their seats and to this day still have the same seats in McKale Center.

When Coach Snowden arrived, this group of twelve couples reached out to assist the Wildcat basketball program during the Snowden era. The Schroeders became members of the family program, as forward Jay Geldmacher was a part of their family. Don, a very successful local attorney, also did legal work for the Snowden family as well as the Olson family. Don remembers, "Fred and Maye [Mrs. Snowden] would throw these great parties at their home to get the community involved."

The community support came in handy when the Snowdens were denied the ability to purchase a home because they were black. The community rallied behind the Snowden family and overturned a controversial law, and a house was built on East Fifth Street for the Snowden family.

As Don said emphatically, "Absolutely Fred brought basketball to Tucson and made Tucson a Basketball Town."

Within one year Coach Snowden was named the 1973 Man of the Year in Tucson. UA basketball tickets were now a hot commodity. Schaefer added, "The people of Tucson had never seen that quality of basketball before, and it was a turn-on." Strack said, "Freddy became the focal point of the entire athletic department."

Arizona basketball has a long and great history, but all of a sudden the University of Arizona became a basketball school, and Tucson became a basketball town.

CHAPTER 4

THE 1973–1974
SEASON

Money returned to the desert for his sophomore season knowing that "all I wanted to do was win." With the addition of front court players like Jerome Gladney and Bob Elliott, as well as Pennsylvania all-everything player Herman Harris, Money knew the program was poised for a run at a championship. "Everything had always been about Arizona State, but we were looking to distinguish the UA from Arizona State. I had the utmost confidence in my ability, and I knew what my team could do. We were going to turn it all around."

Eric Money and Coach Snowden could have their moments. "At times we could be like two bulls in the room, but we were always on the same page really. Coach was always thinking about what was best for you. He was always my best friend," Money remembers. "The constant criticism that Snowden was not an X-and-O coach was just unfair. Let's face it, if you don't have talent, you won't win anything. They go hand in hand,

1973–1974 Arizona basketball team. Left to right, front row: Graduate Assistant Coach Dwight Rees, Assistant Coach Ken Maxey, Head Coach Fred Snowden, Assistant Coach Jerry Holmes. Left to right, back row: Ed Sebanski, Gary Harrison, Jim Rappis, Ron Allen, John Bradley, Len Gordy, Dave Burns, Jerome Gladney, Bob Elliott, Bob Aleksa, Al Fleming, Jay Geldmacher, Jim Wakefield, Herman Harris, Coniel Norman, Kent Markle, Steve Kanner, and Eric Money.

and that holds true then, and it holds true now. Back then every game I played in in McKale was sold out. That accomplishment is played down, but if you're getting beat, ain't nobody coming to the games."

The Arizona basketball recruiting class of the 1973–1974 season would be the most successful in school history. There were eight new members of the Arizona basketball family: Bob Elliott, Herman Harris, Len Gordy, Jerome Gladney, Gary Harrison, Jay Geldmacher, Bob Aleksa, and Kent Markle.

Eric Money, Coniel Norman, Jerome Gladney, and Bob Elliott played on a basketball team during the summer of 1972 representing the city of Detroit in a national tournament in Boston, Massachusetts. The favorite was the team from Washington, DC, led by Adrian Dantley, who would go on to a stellar NBA career. The Detroit team also included future pro basketball players Bubbles Hawkins and Tom LaGarde. Detroit won the tournament, averaging an unbelievable 130 points per game. Elliott remembers, "Eric, Corn, Jerome, and I figured if we stayed together and played at Arizona, we could also win an NCAA national championship. For Eric and me, it was another journey as teammates in organized basketball. I doubt if you can find two guys who were teammates in high school [the Detroit team], college [University of Arizona] and the NBA [New Jersey Nets]."

Jerry Holmes, with his East Coast connections, brought Herman Harris and Len Gordy, high school teammates at Chester High School in Pennsylvania, to Arizona. Coach Snowden brought in Jerome Gladney and Gary Harrison from Michigan.

Assistant Coach Ken Maxey joined the staff that year. "Fred brought that sense of mentorship to his coaching," Maxey recalled. "Once Fred got the job at Arizona we went after recruiting 24/7. Wherever the kids were, that's where we went. We were going to take care of you and take care of your son." Maxey knew his role as an assistant coach: "The job of a head coach is to make decisions, an assistant coaches' job is to make suggestions."

The transition for this group of players from the Midwest and the East was not easy. Len Gordy was unhappy, and he wasn't alone. The six-five defensive specialist from Chester, Pennsylvania, quickly had enough of the Arizona desert. "I had never been that much of a minority before. In Tucson there were more Latinos, more Native Americans, and more whites. That was the first thing I noticed when I came here. I hated it. I was calling home every day. I wanted to leave. A lot of us did. We were just homesick kids doing a lot of talking."

Coach Snowden caught wind of their unhappiness. "We were all sort of talking about it. Nobody was really serious, but somehow coach found out. He pulled us all into a room and just blistered us, I mean he really let us have it. He told us that we could leave, every one of us, and that he would put us all on the first thing smoking heading home." That was that, Gordy recalled.

Gordy had not been the star of his high school team; that honor belonged to Herman Harris, who was a high school All-American. After high school Harris had verbally committed to Florida State. Gordy had planned to stay home and play for the local LaSalle University. No one was recruiting them together, as a pair—except Arizona.

Gordy remembers, "We decided to take one more recruiting visit to Tucson." The Fox got them both. "Years later I had a coach tell me that if he had known we wanted to go together he would have recruited us both. But Coach did, and we both changed our minds."

Bob Elliott received over three hundred letters from colleges. "The recruiting process was difficult for me. I had an array of colleges pursuing me. I had inquiries from the Ivy League schools because my family and I did understand and stress academics, from big-time schools like UCLA and Arizona, all the way down to the small Division II and III colleges like Hope College in Holland, Michigan. I needed some structured, quantitative method to effectively differentiate and compare these institutions. So my father and I developed a decision matrix that had ten questions that were separated into five academic and five athletic categories. The one question that was a deal-breaker was if the college did not have an undergraduate accounting program. I knew I wanted to major in accounting at whatever university I would attend."

At that time as a student-athlete you were allowed six official recruiting trips. The recruiting trips Elliott took were to the University of Arizona, the University of Michigan, Michigan State University, the University of Virginia, and the University of Maryland. "I never took my sixth trip because after these five trips I made a decision that it was really down to the University of Arizona and the University of Michigan. Being the Ann Arbor hometown kid, the University of Michigan would have been a very easy transition. Pioneer High School, the high school I attended, my wife attended, and my dad taught at, was right across the street from the Michigan athletic facilities of the football 'Big House' and Crisler Arena. Probably close to 70 percent of my classmates at Pioneer would attend Michigan. My father and mother were Michigan alums. But Coach Snowden and Coach Strack were at Arizona.

"I knew Coach Snowden and the Snowden family from the time I was in the eighth grade when Coach Snowden was the assistant coach at Michigan. Coach Strack was the basketball coach at the University of Michigan when I started to watch college basketball. The first basketball camp I attended as a kid was the Dave Strack Basketball Camp at Concordia College in Ann Arbor. A couple of times as a kid my dad would take me to Michigan basketball games. I remember one time my dad went to the Michigan ticket office to buy tickets and Coach Strack was there. Coach Strack said to my dad, 'Dr. Elliott, I have to have little Bob play for me in college.' Well, it did happen,

1973–1974 coaching staff.
Left to right: Assistant Coach Ken Maxey,
Assistant Coach Jerry Holmes, Head Coach Fred Snowden

but Strack was the athletic director instead of the basketball coach."

Coach Snowden was an icon in Michigan. He was articulate, smooth, educated, and extremely respected as a man and as a basketball coach. When Coach Snowden came to Elliott's house with his assistant coach Jerry Holmes, Elliott knew he wanted to play for him. That in-house visit by a coach would never be forgotten. Holmes said, "Coach and I met with Dr. and Mrs. Elliott, Bob, and his brothers in their living room. The Elliotts had a pet cat, a huge cat, just looming around. I am allergic to cats. This huge cat jumps up on my lap. I would have hung out with that cat if that was what we had to do to get Bob to commit to Arizona."

Elliott's recruiting trip to the University of Arizona occurred during the last day of September and the first days of October of 1972. The weather in Michigan was rainy, and the temperature was dropping toward the freezing mark at night. Tucson was eighty-five and sunny. That was very impressive even for a seventeen-year-old kid. Saturday morning breakfast was attended by Coach Snowden, Assistant Coach Holmes, Assistant Coach Ken Maxey, and President John

OFFICIAL BASKETBALL BOX

Blood Sh... ³³

ARIZONA	FIELD GOALS MADE	ATTD.	FREE THROWS MADE	ATTD.	RE-BOUNDS	ASSTS	PER. FOULS	TOTAL POINTS	TURN OVERS	MINS. PLAYED
R. NORMAN	9	19	1	1	8	3	1	19		30 30
54 FLEMING	6	7	0	0	11	0	5	12	1	32 00
55 ELGLOW	9	13	4	4	19	1	3	22	3	30 00
12 ALLEN	6	13	2	2	2	5	2	14		37 30
14 MONEY	6	12	2	2	2	3	4	14		38 00
24 HARRIS	9	15	2	3	2	1	4	20	1	29 30
15 RAPPIS	0	2	0	0	1	2	0	0		11 30
52 WAKEMAN	0	0	0	0	2	0	2	0		8 00
44 Glodney	0	7	0	0	0	0	1	0		2 00
21 Gordy	0	0	0	0	3	0	0	0		8 00
TOTALS	45	83	11	12	48	15	22	101	5	

PERCENTAGES: FGs: 1st H. _85 %_ 2nd H. _547_ Game ____ Shots Missed ____
FTs: 1st H. _0 %_ 2nd H. _900_ Game ____ Team Rebounds _6_

ILLINOIS	FIELD GOALS MADE	ATTD.	FREE THROWS MADE	ATTD.	RE-BOUNDS	ASSTS	PER. FOULS	TOTAL POINTS	TURN OVERS	MINS. PLAYED
32 SCHMIDT	12	23	3	6	11	8	4	27		36 45
33 TUCKER	5	15	0	0	3	1	4	10		38 00
53 RHCES	4	5	2	2	5	1	3	10		25 30
11 ROBERTS	2	6	2	4	7	3	2	6		33 30
24 DAWSON	8	22	4	5	7	1	0	20		40 00
25 DEPUTY	0	3	0	0	3		1	0	1	8 50
15 CARMICHAEL	2	3	2	2	3		2	6		14 30
20 GRAFF	0	0	1	2	1	1	0	1		2 00
43 FARNUM	0	0	0	0	0	1	2	0		2 00
30 WENTE	0	2	0	0	1	1	0	0		
TOTALS	33	79	14	21	31	8	18	80		

PERCENTAGES: FGs: 1st H. _38.5 %_ 2nd H. _417_ Game ____ Shots Missed ____
FTs: 1st H. _37.3 %_ 2nd H. _667_ Game ____ Team Rebounds _2_

OFFICIALS: BROWN - PHILLIPS SCORE BY PERIODS

TIMER: _____ 13458

	1	2	3	4	OT	OT	
ARIZONA	36						101
ILLINOIS	51						80

Arizona vs. Illinois, November 30, 1973,
official basketball box score

Schaefer. Elliott recalled, "it was great to see Coach Maxey. Coach Maxey had been the star point guard for the Michigan basketball team in the late 1960s. He was also my counselor at the Dave Strack basketball camp.

"I was able to get answers for all of the academic and athletic questions I had. Later that spring I remember my press conference where I announced I would be attending the University of Arizona. Everyone in Ann Arbor expected me to attend the University of Michigan, as I was not only the local kid but my parents were Michigan alums. My dad even played drums in the Michigan band back in the late 1940s and early 1950s. The University of Arizona band director, Jack Lee, who wrote the fight song 'Bear Down, Arizona,' was in charge of the percussion section of the Michigan band when my father was at Michigan. But I was coming out west to Tucson to join Coach Snowden and Coach Strack."

Dave Sitton, the long-time University of Arizona TV broadcaster, was a freshman baseball player at the UA during the 1973–1974 season. The basketball players and the baseball players both lived in the Graham Hall dormitory. The basketball players were on the first floor, and the baseball players were on the second floor. Dave loved music and this love of music helped to develop a bond between Dave and the basketball players, who were mostly black. The University of Arizona did not have many black students, and many of the black students were in fact the student athletes. Part of Dave's cultural experience in Graham Hall involved sharing music. "I wish I had a dollar for every time I was awakened by the soul music of the Isley Brothers song 'Who's that Lady,'" Dave said.

The season started against the University of Illinois of the Big Ten Conference. "Just like any true freshman would be, I was psyched. I knew my role," Elliott said. With the four returning starters who were now sophomores, Elliott needed to blend in. "I played center that year, and I was needed to rebound, block shots, defend the middle, and I was the third option on offense after Eric and Coniel. We beat Illinois that day in McKale Center."

That next day the team flew over to Los Angeles to play USC. Now in the program, Elliott was listed as six foot ten. "I was not then, nor have I ever been six feet ten inches tall. I was probably a legitimate six seven and a half at that time as a freshman at the UA. But nobody knew the difference with eight inches of afro on my head."

USC had a center named John Lambert. He was also listed at six foot ten in the game program. "That night I found out that just as some players are listed taller than they really are in the program like I was, some players are listed shorter than they are. John Lampert was probably closer to seven feet tall. So I go to midcourt for the jump ball to start the game, and I was looking up to this guy. I had to back off the center circle because it really took me by surprise."

Facilities in the WAC conference were a mixed bag. Brigham Young and Utah had both recently built tributes to the love of the game. The Marriott Center in Provo could house twenty-two thousand. The Utes' Huntsman Arena was smaller (fifteen thousand) but a palace. The facility at Colorado State in Fort Collins was strictly utilitarian, just what you might expect from a town that began as a military outpost. Down south, New Mexico's Pit was known as one of the toughest places to play in the west. In El Paso, the fans and the facilities were nearly as intimidating as the man they represented: head coach Don Haskins.

Then there was the University of Wyoming in Laramie. Laramie had a very high altitude that made it hard to breathe. The gym at the University of Wyoming was a barn that also was used for rodeos. "The floor was sawdust, and it smelled like horse manure," Rappis recalled. "One game the fans were throwing beer cans at us. The official kicked the beer can off the court and then handed me the ball."

Mats were laid from the locker room to the basketball court so the players would not step on anything that was left from the rodeo. The court was an elevated portable floor that would go on top of the dirt. As Russell Brown from the 1977–1981 teams said, "Not too many guys would dive for a ball and take the chance of going off the court and land on something."

One of the hardest road trips in the WAC Conference was to play New Mexico in The Pit and a day or two later travel to and play the University of Texas at El Paso (UTEP). In Albuquerque they really love the Lobos and are very excitable fans. But the UTEP game was one Elliott would never forget. UTEP played a style of basketball that year where they would hold onto the ball, stall, and really slow down the pace of the game. There was not a shot clock in those days. This made them a very dangerous opponent. Earlier that year in Tucson this strategy worked, as UTEP took an early lead, and Arizona was never able to come back. *Sports Illustrated* magazine interviewed the Arizona team later that year, and point guard Eric Money made the comment that they did not play basketball at UTEP. UTEP was waiting for Arizona big time after reading that article.

The place was packed and rowdy an hour and a half before the game. Many things were said back and forth between the crowd and the players, and the situation became extremely volatile. UTEP had a very cozy, small gym similar to Bear Down Gymnasium. Behind the basket their fans were right there next to the court. Elliott said, "On a free throw attempt by a UTEP player, I felt something burn and singe me on my left leg. I looked down and saw a penny on the floor. I looked into the crowd, and a guy just smiled at me and gave me a few gestures. We beat El Paso that day, and it felt great."

That year Arizona played against some very good big men who went on to enjoy great NBA careers, including Maurice Lucas at Marquette and Robert Parish at Centenary. But the one big man everybody was talking about was Ron 'the Rock' Kennedy at ASU. Elliott remembered, "The week of the ASU game on Monday, Eric Money told me that I was going to have the ball all game long. For that game I would not be the third option, but I was the first option. I took a ridiculous amount of shots that day. I had twenty field goal attempts and twenty free throw attempts. We beat ASU that day."

Another exciting game that year was against Kansas State. It was a very close game. The guy Elliott was guarding had just made a basket near the end of the game to tie the score. "I felt awful like I had let our team down. Coach Snowden called timeout to set up the final play. Instead of inbounding the ball to our point guard Eric Money, the ball was to be inbounded to me to bring it down the floor. I had Eric and Jimmy Rappis on the wings and Al Fleming and Coniel Norman on the baseline. I was to penetrate, create a mismatch, and pass it to one of them for the final shot. Being eighteen years old, I felt this was my chance to make amends for my failure of letting my man

Arizona vs. Arizona State, February 2, 1974, Bob Elliott posting up Ron "the Rock" Kennedy of Arizona State

score. So I received the pass, dribbled down the floor, and took the shot just as I crossed over half court." The shot had so much arc on it that it was in the air when the horn went off and still had not gone through the basket when the horn stopped. Arizona won the game on that shot.

Because of the excitement of Arizona basketball with Coach Fred Snowden and the Kiddie Korp, Channel 11, under the guidance of Gene Adelstein, broadcasted all of the Arizona basketball games. Some of the games would be on tape delay. So after the game, the many ticket holders at McKale Center, the players and the coaches, would go home and watch the replay on Channel 11. Once the Doobie Brothers started the broadcast with the song "China Grove," it was game time. With Gene Adelstein as the play-by-play announcer and Eric Steffens providing the color, the commitment of Channel 11 added to Tucson being a basketball town.

But there is more to the story of Channel 11. At that time the transmitter for Channel 11 was in Nogales, Arizona. Therefore the television signal in Tucson was inconsistent. Many times during a game broadcast a viewer would have to adjust the TV antenna to keep watching the game. But in Nogales the basketball games were extremely clear. Arizona basketball was huge in Nogales, Arizona, and Nogales, Sonora, Mexico. Elliott remembers, "We were shopping on the other side of the border in Nogales, Sonora. The kids and adults were coming from all directions, out of stores, everywhere. It was crazy like I was a rock star, except I could not understand what they were saying. We went into this Curio Shop named Honest Johns. Honest John spoke very good English. He asked if I understood what they were calling me. I told him I did not have a clue. They were calling me Pajarito, which in Spanish means Birdie. Sometimes they would call me Pajarito Grande or Big Bird which was my nickname. To this day I can go to Nogales, cross the border, and hear Pajarito, and I love it."

In 1974 the NCAA tournament had only 32 participants whereas now there are 65 participants. Arizona's record that year was 19–7, and they finished in second place in the WAC Conference. But the rule that year was that if you hosted an NCAA tournament, you had to either play in the NCAA tournament or not at all in any postseason tournament. To be able to play in the NCAA tournament Arizona had to win the WAC conference. But hosting a NCAA tournament would be great exposure for Arizona with this new, beautiful arena, McKale Center. Arizona came in second in the WAC Conference that year, and therefore they were not allowed to play in a postseason tournament.

Elliott said, "I remember sitting in McKale Center watching the NCAA tournament triple overtime game between Bill Walton and the UCLA Bruins and the University of Dayton Flyers, led by the freshman superstar Johnny Davis from Detroit's Murray-Wright High School. They were playing this game on our McKale Center floor."

McKale Center was state of the art, with the latest and greatest amenities, including a rubber floor. The rubber floor looked great on TV. The selling point was to drop a quarter on the floor, the quarter would bounce way up in the air. The traditional wooden floor could not do this trick. But that rubber floor was rough on the knees and ankles of the players. Every time a player would stop, the rubber on the bottom of their sneakers would meet the rubber of the floor, and there would not be any

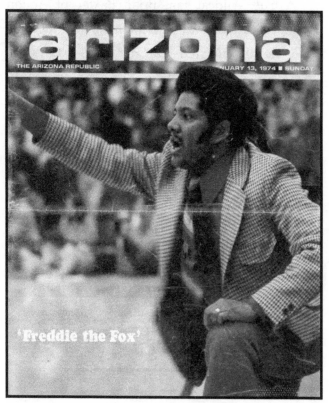

Coach Fred Snowden in McKale Center, 1974

give. Players' knees and ankles took all of the stress every time they stopped, planted, or cut during a practice or game.

A true Wildcat fan, Brian Baxter of Action Communications, was a school kid during this time. He remembered that McKale Center had a special smell and that even today you can go into McKale Center and still smell that unique smell. "That is so true" concurred Elliott, "especially that elevator by the McKale ticket office. I can close my eyes and know immediately I am in that elevator even today."

McKale Center and its unique smell has stayed around for over forty years. The history and mystique of McKale Center is more than what happened on the basketball floor.

Arizona versus Texas Tech basketball program,
December 22, 1973

CHAPTER 5

THE 1974–1975
SEASON

This was a tough year for Arizona basketball—a transition year. First, the leading scorers from last year's team, Eric Money and Coniel Norman, left the University of Arizona to pursue a professional basketball career by declaring financial hardship to the NBA. "The options were slimmer at that time. The rules on hardship were different. You couldn't test the waters like you can today. It was a tough call, loyalty to the team versus going pro and helping your family," said Money.

Money spoke about a deciding factor for him being longevity in the game and his size as a point guard. "The constant possibility of injuries shortening your career takes some of your options away," he said. "If I'm going to get hurt, I'm going to get paid for it."

Believe it or not, the pro game could be a less physical place for a point guard with Money's talents. "In college I would take it to the basket, challenge people. I was only going so far into the

The 1974–1975 Arizona basketball team, front row, left to right: Graduate Assistant Coach Dave Strack Jr., Jim Rappis, Steve Kanner, Gary Harrison, Gilbert Myles, Marc Holt, Tom Ehlmann, Tim Marshall, Assistant Coach Jerry Holmes. Back row, left to right: Assistant Coach Ken Maxey, Herman Harris, Bob Elliott, Bob Aleksa, Jerome Gladney, Jay Geldmacher, Phil Taylor, Mitch Jones, Al Fleming, Len Gorday, Dave Burns, Ernie Valenzuela, Head Coach Fred Snowden.

paint (at the professional level), and then I was going to pull up and shoot the ball. The professional game for a point guard is basically played foul line to foul line," he said. With the NBA's twenty-four-second clock there is much more running, all of which fit into his talents.

Second, both starting guards needed surgery at the end of the season. Freshman point guard Gilbert Myles had knee surgery, and shooting guard Jim Rappis had back surgery. To compensate, Arizona made a few adjustments to the lineup. Elliott moved to the small forward, and Jerome Gladney moved to the center position. With Eric Money gone, Elliott now became the first option on offense, with Al Fleming moving up from the fourth option to the second option. That year Elliott averaged 23.3 points per game, and Fleming averaged 19.8 points per game. Arizona had a decent year even though the third-place finish in the WAC Conference would be the worst finish the 1973–1974 recruiting class would have in their four years as Wildcats. The final record was 22-7.

Luckily that year the NCAA started a new tournament called the Commissioners Tournament, held at Freedom Hall in Louisville, Kentucky. As the third place team in the WAC Conference, Arizona was invited. Elliott said, "We made it to the championship game against Drake that would be televised live on NBC Sports. For a nineteen-year-old that was a major thrill. During the warm-ups I saw the announcer Sonny Hill, an announcer that I had seen on TV before. But the highlight was in the locker room before the game. Needless to say we were all very nervous to go on national TV. Dave Burns, a reserve forward for us, before the game said he could not find his jersey. He was really upset. Then he looked down and realized he had it on. We all broke out in laughter, and that helped break the ice and stop the pre-game jitters."

This was also the first year that Ernesto Valenzuela, a new freshman on campus and a product of Tucson High School, would begin an eight-year run as the team manager. He was known as Big Ern, and he always kept everyone loose. Big Ern had the gift of comedy. He was also the keeper of the team meal money, so he was the best friend of the players. For young men who were always hungry, Big Ern was the guy to see.

Len Gordy stated, "This is when I knew we were big time. We were at an elementary school, making an appearance or something. This little kid shot a fade-away shot that he made, and I heard him say, 'Basket by Herm the Germ!' Then another kid pulled down a rebound, and he said, 'Big Bird!' We had that kind of impact on the children in the community. Coach Snowden endured a lot of slights to his coaching abilities. The constant suggestion that he was a recruiter and not a true coach stung. "That's like the guy that says the black kids are athletic and talented and gifted, and the white players are always heady and smart. The guy went to his grave a coach. He took a hole in the ground called McKale and he filled it."

Jackie Baxter Armijo made a drawing of Wilber the Wildcat and as the 1974-75 basketball team arrived at Tucson International Airport from a road trip, had the players sign the drawing.

Drawing of Wilber the Wildcat by Jackie Baxter Armijo, signed by the 1974–1975 Arizona basketball team

CHAPTER 6

THE 1975–1976
SEASON

This was the year for Arizona basketball. Everybody was healthy, and they went back to their regular lineup with Elliott at center. But they had a tough time getting started early in the year. For the 1973–1974 recruiting class, the record of 24-9 was the worst record of the four years, yet they had the most postseason success that year. Arizona won the WAC championship that year and played in the NCAA tournament. Jerry Pimm, the head basketball coach at the University of Utah, said Arizona ran the "Monopoly offense," with hotels on Boardwark and Park Place (referring to Fleming and Elliott).

The first game in the NCAA tournament was against Georgetown University at the ASU Arena in Tempe. "At the time we did not know the true significance of this game," Elliott remembers. This was the first time a black coach had his team in the NCAA tournament. Actually, both teams had black head coaches: Fred Snowden of Arizona and

The 1975–1976 Arizona basketball team, front row, left to right: Jay Geldmacher, Jerome Gladney, Bob Elliott, Jim Rappis, Head Coach Fred Snowden, Al Fleming, Len Gordy, Herman Harris, Bob Aleksa, Gary Harrison. Back row, left to right: Assistant Coach Ken Maxey, Graduate Assistant Coach Steve Kanner, Sylvester Maxey, Greg Lloyd, Tim Marshall, Tom Ehlmann, Brian Jung, Phil Taylor, Larry Demic, Mitch Jones, Ron Fuller, Gilbert Myles, Ernie Valenzuela, trainer Dennis Murphy, Assistant Coach Dave Toney.

John Thompson of Georgetown. So one of these two would be the first black head coach to win an NCAA tournament game. Arizona went on to win that game and advanced to the NCAA tournament Sweet Sixteen.

The next opponent was the number three ranked Running Rebels of UNLV coached by Jerry "Tark the Shark" Tarkanian. Arizona won the game 114–109 in overtime.

Now the Cats would become the first Arizona basketball team to play in the Elite Eight of the NCAA tournament. Roommates Fleming and Elliott could not go to sleep that night after beating UNLV, as they were too hyped about the opportunity to play UCLA for a chance to go to the Final Four. The game would be played at Pauley Pavilion, the home of the UCLA Bruins, in Los Angeles. Elliott said, "I always wondered how UCLA would be allowed to host an NCAA regional with their history of all of the NCAA championships that they had recently won."

Because it was the NCAA Western Regional game, it was the last of the four regional final games to be played in the 1976 NCAA tournament. The other three teams to advance to the Final Four

NCAA
Pre-Regional
Playoffs

March 13, 1976

Pepperdine vs. Memphis State
Arizona vs. Georgetown D.C.

Arizona vs. Georgetown basketball program, March 13, 1976

were already determined. It was a close game until a timeout was called with 5:52 left to play. Arizona came out flat after the timeout, and UCLA went on to win the game and advance to the Final Four. It was a good run and a good year.

After the success of the Elite Eight season, Snowden was the most sought-out celebrity in town. The bandwagon was in full effect. "Everybody wanted a piece of Fred, and he couldn't be everywhere. It [McKale] was the place to be, and he was the person to be around," Maxey remembers. "I thought he handled a lot of it well. He may have been a little too much into himself at times—the television show, the articles. A lot of coaches were beginning to make money on the side . . . but Coach had a vision and a plan, and he knew how to handle kids."

Al Fleming finished the year as the UA career scoring leader and rebound leader. Fleming also finished as the third and last UA basketball player to average a double-double during their career at 15.5 points per game and 10.4 rebounds per game. Fleming is still the UA career rebound leader.

A controversial topic has been and probably will always be the power of athletics in the economic arena. This Arizona basketball team, by going to the Elite Eight of the NCAA basketball tournament, proved the power of athletics in the economic world. At the time the University of Arizona was in the process of building the new library located across from McKale Center. Unlike some buildings, the library would not be eligible for a bond program to fund the project. It was, as Dr. Schaefer said, "pay as you go." Not only did the University of Arizona receive additional monies from the Cats' appearance in the NCAA tournament, but the goodwill created with the alumni would help the University of Arizona development officers to cultivate relationships with the alumni and attract donations. Also the Arizona Board of Regents were very happy with the additional positive publicity for the state of Arizona and were more supportive toward the library project. The new library was completed across from McKale Center and is still serving students today.

Bob Elliott attempts a free throw against UNLV, 1976

Al Fleming and Coach Fred Snowden, 1973

CHAPTER 7

THE 1976–1977
SEASON

This was the most successful year record-wise for the recruiting class of 1973–1974, with twenty-one wins and six losses. But it was also the most disappointing year. Arizona did make the NCAA tournament for a second year in a row, which was a great accomplishment. But after the success of last year's appearance in the Elite Eight, expectations were high. Arizona lost in the first round to Southern Illinois, who was led by their sharpshooting guard Mike "Stinger" Glenn.

Phil Taylor replaced the graduated Al Fleming in the starting lineup, and Elliott would move over to the power forward position. Elliott's childhood friend Gary Harrison moved into the starting point guard position that helped his transition to power forward. "Gary and I had been playing basketball since the eighth grade in pickup games at the University of Michigan Intramural Building, so we knew each other extremely well," Elliott said.

Another highlight (or lowlight) was a chance

1976-77 UNIVERSITY OF ARIZONA WILDCATS

Front row (left to right): Bob Aleksa, Jerome Gladney, Len Gordy, Herman Harris, Coach Fred Snowden, Bob Elliott, Tom Ehlmann, Gary Harrison, and Phil Taylor. *Standing (left to right):* Ken Maxey, assistant coach; Phil Gaines, equipment manager; Steve Kanner, graduate assistant coach; Tommy Williams, Greg Lloyd, Tim Marshall, Jay Geldmacher, Kenny Davis, Brian Jung, Larry Demic, Mitch Jones, Ron Fuller, Joe Nehls, Gilbert Myles, David Leigh, trainer; Ernie Valenzuela, manager; and John Sneed, assistant coach.

for many of the Detroit area Arizona basketball players to go back home to the Detroit area and play the University of Detroit. Detroit was coached by the current well-known ESPN sportscaster Dick Vitale. Arizona played Detroit the year before and put a major spanking on them to the tune of 106–76. Al Fleming scored 33 of his 41 points in the second half to set a McKale Center record for points scored in a half that still stands today. Coach Snowden was presented with the key to the City of Detroit to recognize him not only for being the first high-profile black head basketball coach in Division I of the NCAA, but also for reaching the Elite Eight the year before.

Detroit built this year's game up as the big payback for the loss Arizona put on them the year before. They said they were going to run Arizona into the ground, but instead Detroit came out in a stall offense and played a 1-3-1 zone defense to also slow down the tempo of the game. In the end it worked for Detroit, as they won 70–68.

Then there was the exhibition game against the Russian Nationals. This game would be televised nationally, so this was an excellent opportunity for the Arizona basketball program to receive national exposure. In 1972 the sting of the USA basketball controversial loss to the Russian Olympic team was still on the minds of many Americans. On the ticket stub the game was publicized as "The Russians Are Coming." This game was part of a goodwill mission between the Tucson Jewish Community Council and the Soviet Jewry Commission. It was an exhibition game, so it did not count toward the team record, nor would the individual statistics be counted.

But the crazy part about this game had nothing to do with the game itself. The normal protocol for a game involving two different countries is to have the players line up across from each other and then formally present a gift to an opposing player as a gesture of goodwill. Then the national anthem of each country would be played and observed. First "The Star-Spangled Banner" was played. Then a song came on that was supposed to be the Russian national anthem. The Russian players were moving around during the song and not really paying attention. After the game it was determined that the song was not the Russian national anthem but rather the Russian Red Army fight song. That would be like playing "Bear Down,

Arizona vs. Moscow Red Army program and ticket stub,
March 6, 1977

Arizona" instead of "The Star-Spangled Banner." Good thing this debacle did not start a World War.

None of the players nor the community knew the kind of unnecessary pressure Coach Snowden and his family dealt with on a daily basis. One day in practice Coach was in an awful mood. The players had the kind of open relationship with Coach Snowden where they could call him out if something was not right or not going well. But this day Coach did not want to hear it. Elliott, as he always did, pushed Snowden's buttons.

Elliott remembers, "Coach said for everyone to take a break. 'Elliott, meet me in my office Now!' So Coach and I went upstairs to his office. He told me to sit in his chair and open up his bottom right-hand drawer. There was a bunch of mail in the drawer. Coach said, 'Go ahead. You are the Academic All-American. Read.' It was all hate mail and included death threats. One I remember distinctly that this person said he would kill Coach with his white shoes on. I looked up and apologized to Coach that I had no idea what he was going through. Coach said, 'Now you know, so if some days I am not in a good mood, you might understand why.'"

Stacey Snowden was an elementary school

ARIZONA WILDCAT BASKETBALL
1977 NCAA PARTICIPANT
Three Straight Seasons of 20 or More Wins

Fred Snowden
Head Basketball Coach

Dr. John P. Schaefer
President

Dave Strack
Director of Athletics

The University
of Arizona
Welcomes you to the
Basketball Awards
Banquet Honoring
The 1976-77 Team
March 21

1977 Arizona basketball banquet program

child when Coach Snowden accepted the head coaching position at the University of Arizona. Stacey remembers, "I never had a normal childhood. As the other classmates went out for recess, sometimes I had to stay in the classroom due to the threats. Periodically I was not even allowed to go outside our own home because of the threats. But my family and I supported Dad unconditionally in his profession and his quest for success."

The recruiting class of 1973–1974 (Bob Elliott, Herman Harris, Len Gordy, Jerome Gladney, Gary Harrison, Jay Geldmacher, Bob Aleksa, and Tucson Saguaro's own Kent Markle) would finish their four years with a home record of 59–2 including forty-five home wins in a row. A great accomplishment by any standard.

CHAPTER 8

THE PAC-10
CONFERENCE

D r. Schaefer was the catalyst for the move to the Pacific 10 Conference. He and his colleague at USC drove this opportunity for the University of Arizona and Arizona State University. It was not a slam dunk with the Arizona Board of Regents, Northern Arizona University, or even Arizona State University. But for Schaefer it was a necessary academic and athletic move to associate the University of Arizona with respected college institutions.

During his four years in the program, Len Gordy came to be known as a cerebral player, a coach on the floor. "I always knew what Coach wanted. When Bob and Al were yelling at the guards and Herm and Rap were yelling at the bigs, Coach would say 'Lenny, talk to them.' And I would have to settle it. I wasn't going to allow things to go down that way if I knew Coach didn't want it to," Gordy said.

Upon graduation, Gordy had four years in

a successful major college program, a degree in communications and no immediate career goals. "By the end of my senior year I only needed two classes. I figured I would graduate and get a job working in radio or TV. Then Coach Maxey left and Coach Holmes started pushing me for a job as an assistant," remembers Gordy. It was another area where Snowden showed leadership and an eye toward trends, Gordy says now. "Back then nobody had really started the trend of creating continuity and hiring their ex-players, whereas nowadays that is fairly common. Not until I started my own coaching career did I truly appreciate the toughness of guys like Jimmy Rappis and Al Fleming. Nobody was ever going to out-work them." From that time on, 'defensive specialist' Gordy became 'coach' Gordy.

Larry Demic, who would become the first University of Arizona basketball player to be drafted by the NBA in the first round, remembers, "Going to the PAC meant you had powerful programs like UCLA in basketball and USC in football. The PAC was big time. There were better athletes on the competitors' teams. The PAC was a better publicized conference compared to the WAC. The PAC had recognized national championships. The teams from the PAC dominated the national scene. How can we compete with these guys? Coach Snowden never said this directly, but I sensed that we were concerned about falling on our face that first year in the PAC."

Joe Nehls, the sharp shooting guard on that team remembers the bumper stickers that read, "Back the Cats, WAC to PAC."

Russell Brown, who holds the Arizona assists records for a single game, for a season, and for a career said, "I came to Arizona to play in the Pac-10. I wanted to go to UCLA, was recruited by UCLA, but I was their second choice behind Arte Green of New York. I had an uncle who went to Wayne State University in Detroit with Coach Snowden, and that relationship helped with my choice to attend Arizona. I wanted to be close to LA, but I also wanted warm weather." After playing at UA, Brown was a district manager for Baskin-Robbins reporting to Coach Snowden, who was an executive with the corporate office of Baskin-Robbins following his coaching career. Brown remembers Coach Snowden fondly. "Coach was a great mentor on and off the court as well as while I was in school and after I left the UA."

Robbie Dosty, who was drafted in 1981 by the Golden State Warriors, remembers Coach Snowden's unique but effective methods of teaching. "I can remember one instance when coming out of a game I'd made a dumb mistake and was being replaced. Coach met me near the end of the scorer's table and asked me, 'Boy, have you lost your mind? If you ever do a dumb thing like that again, I'll jump right into that number twenty-one on your chest!' I looked at him and [was] completely lost the entire time, not because of what he was saying to me because that's the way coaches' talk. But more so because the entire time he was saying this to me, he was smiling and nodding as though we were having a pleasant conversation. I couldn't help but think, 'This man's crazy!' This was my first experience of this nature with coach. He told me later and I later learned that type of episode was important to him—very important to him. He told me, and I heard him say it on many other occasions, 'I will not embarrass you in front of the crowd at McKale.' He did all he could not to embarass a player in front of the crowd, and I cannot remember a moment that he ever did!

"A second time, I grew a beard and mustache which attached. Coach came over and stood by me. Smiling, he asked almost with approval, 'I see you're growing a beard.' I was a little unsure, so I agreed with him. He then asked, completely stone-faced, "Who the [heck] are you, Fu-Manchu? Shave that [stuff] off your face tonight!' Which I did. Before practice the next day, he had me come into his locker area in the locker room and explained, 'Some of those people that sit in the stands will be the same people you one day seek out and ask for a job. They don't know you. They know what they see of you. Don't give anyone a reason to judge you negatively without knowing you. Make sense?' It did. I said, 'Yes, sir,' left his office, and never grew a beard again!"

Lorenzo Romar, presently the head basket-ball coach at the University of Washington, has memories of Coach Snowden during Romar's collegiate playing days at the University of Washington. "Coach Snowden's Arizona teams were always very disciplined. You knew going into the game that Russell Brown was going to have

Pac-10 game Coach Fred Snowden (right) and
Assistant Coach Len Gordy (left), 1979

the ball, Joe Nehls was the shooter on the wings, and Larry Demic was going to be in the post. My coaching career is a product of the success of a coach like Fred Snowden."

A significant and memorable moment came during that 1978–1979 first year in the Pac-10 when Arizona beat UCLA and USC in McKale Center one January weekend.

Russell Brown said, "I had that day circled on my calendar when I arrived at Arizona."

Larry Demic remembers, "That was an exciting weekend. My dad flew in for the weekend, and it would be the first time my dad would be able to watch me play. UCLA had a loaded roster with a few All-Americans like David Greenwood, Kiki Vanderwege, solid guard play from Roy Hamilton and Brad Holland, and a nice small forward in James Wilkes. Practice went well that week. We worked hard that week. We were laser-focused. We knew we had to play together, but we had our work cut out for us."

Joe Nehls remembers that week vividly. "The week before (the UCLA and USC games) we went to Oregon and Oregon State and lost. Actually, Oregon State beat us badly by thirty-six points. It

Left to right, Robbie Dosty, Assistant Coach Len Gordy, Assistant Coach Mike Frink,
Head Coach Fred Snowden, 1981

was a long trip home after that game. We knew we were better than that. Near the end of the UCLA game, Arizona was winning. Then we went into a stall offense, and UCLA came back to go ahead. I hit a jumper from the corner to tie the game. John Smith was fouled on the next possession and missed the first free throw but made the second free throw to put us up by one. David Greenwood, who was guarded by John Belobraydic, attempted a last-second shot that missed, and we won the game. The crowd rushed the floor. It was crazy."

The schedule had a long, unconventional break, as four days later USC would come to Tucson. They were led by Cliff Robinson, who would be a lottery pick with the New Jersey Nets after that year. After the UCLA win, the Cats had a lot of confidence going into the USC game. But the best part was a marketing scheme for free spaghetti sponsored by a local restaurant if the Cats won. Needless to say, there was free spaghetti for all in McKale Center that day. After the game the crowd rushed the floor again just like after the UCLA win. Demic called it "definitely the highlight of my college career." That UCLA/USC weekend put Demic on the national

Snowden statement

I am relinquishing my position as Head Basketball Coach at the University of Arizona effective at the conclusion of this 1981-82 Basketball Season.

I have been offered and I have accepted a position in Athletic Administration at the University of Arizona effective at the conclusion of this season.

Coach Fred Snowden's March 1982 letter of resignation

radar screen and significantly increased his NBA draft stock.

At the end of the 1981–82 season, Coach Snowden announced he would be resigning as the head basketball coach to accept a position in athletic administration at Arizona.

Celebration of the Life

of

Fredrick Snowden

April 3, 1936   January 17, 1994

Saturday
January 22, 1994
11:00 A.M.

McKale Center
University of Arizona
Tucson, Arizona

Fred Snowden memorial service program, January 22, 1994

CHAPTER 9

ARIZONA BASKETBALL, AFTER 1983—LUTE OLSON, SEAN MILLER

The true cornerstone of any great athletic program is coaching longevity—a coach or series of coaches whose concepts and visions conquer the whims of time.

After a one-year stint with Ben Lindsey as the head coach at Arizona, athletic director Dr. Cedric Dempsey went to Dr. Henry Koffler, the president of the university, with a proposal to hire Lute Olson, who was the head basketball coach at Iowa. Olson would coach the Cats for the next twenty-four years, from 1983 until 2007, including the one and only national championship for Arizona basketball in 1997.

Olson and his family liked the warm climate in Tucson. Olson remembered Tucson fondly, as he used to travel there for BCI high school tournaments. He liked the challenge to turn the basketball program around. Olson said, "The basketball program had not gone to a postseason tournament in the last six years, and the last team (coached by Ben Lindsey) had a record of 4-24."

Olson said, "The key to our turning the program around was that first recruiting class that included Pete Williams, Steve Kerr, and Eddie Smith. Our first practice was scheduled for two and a half hours, and we went for four hours." As with many of the teams Olson coached, team chemistry was big. "If Pete Williams does not come to Arizona, Sean Elliott would not have committed to Arizona." Sean liked what he saw with Pete, Steve, and Eddie and committed to Arizona. Sean Elliott (no relation to Bob Elliott) played from 1985–1989 and became the first Arizona basketball player to be named a National Player of the Year.

In Olson's first year, the team had an 11–17 record. The 1984–1985 squad had a record of 21–10 and was invited to the NCAA tournament. That was the beginning of twenty-three consecutive NCAA tournament appearances, eleven Pac-10 championships, four Final Four appearances, and a national championship (1997) under Olson.

In the late 1980s, 1990s, and 2000s during the Lute Olson era, Arizona was known as Point Guard U. With such point guards during this era as Steve Kerr, Damon Stoudamire, Mike Bibby, Jason Terry, and Jason Gardner, that nickname was well deserved. In fact, of the four retired Arizona basketball jerseys, three belong to point guards (Kerr, Bibby, and Gardner). The other retired jersey belongs to Sean Elliott. But two point guards during the Fred Snowden era, Eric Money and Russell Brown, should be added to this list of the greatest point guards in the history of Arizona basketball. Then there is Jim Rappis also from the Snowden era, whose leadership, toughness, shooting ability and basketball IQ could also be included on this list of outstanding point guards.

After Coach Olson retired, Arizona had a couple of one-year coaching stints under Kevin O'Neill and Russ Pennell that extended the NCAA tournament participation streak to twenty-five years in a row.

Then Sean Miller was named the head basketball coach of Arizona. Miller, in an interview for this book said, "I never met Coach Snowden, but I know he got a lot of things started at Arizona. Arizona was attractive because if you look at the longevity of Coach Olson's career, there had to be something special about Arizona. My goal is to embrace the past players and teams. We want to be known as a players program. We want to respect the past players and welcome them back to our program. I want players to look at the Arizona program with immense pride. As we build our brand, we want the current players to know who has done it before. How many people come to the game to watch. The electricity in McKale. Tradition is the biggest thing we sell to recruits about Arizona. Tucson might be the biggest college town in the country."

After a 16–15 record in Miller's first year (2009–10), the NCAA tournament streak ended. In his second year (2010-11), Arizona went 30–8, made it to the Elite Eight, and was one shot away from the Final Four. "The key was that first recruiting class that included Derrick Williams," Miller said.

The 2011–12 team went 23–12 and participated in the NIT tournament. The 2012–13 team returned to the NCAA tournament and participated in the Sweet Sixteen. They were led by Solomon Hill, a four year letterman, who would be a first round draft pick of the Indiana Pacers.

ACKNOWLEDGMENTS

It is my honor to have this opportunity to express thanks and gratitude. I am thankful to Coach Fred Snowden for convincing me to leave the comfortable surroundings of Ann Arbor, Michigan and to take a risk to attend the University of Arizona in Tucson. I am grateful for the warm reception the Tucson community has given me, as well as the warm reception the community has given many Wildcat basketball players who have had the opportunity to wear with pride the red and blue. I honor and have the utmost respect for Dr. John Schaefer and Coach Dave Strack for being visionaries and hiring an African American basketball coach in 1972.

I appreciate Mrs. Maye Snowden and their children, Stacey and Chuck, for enduring and experiencing unbelievable trials and tribulations as they supported their father and our coach as he pursued his coaching dream.

I would like to thank Roderick Gary for his contributions to this book.

This book would not have been possible without my wife, four children, ten grandchildren, and parents, who have been inspirational and have given me love and support throughout my journey as a basketball player, businessman, and community advocate.

Last but not least, I want to thank God for his many blessings while guiding me through my life experiences.

Tucson became a basketball town in 1972 and has been a basketball town ever since. I leave you with those magical words all Wildcats live by: "Bear Down."

Bob "Big Bird" Elliott
University of Arizona Basketball
1973–1977

PHOTO CREDITS

COVER PHOTO

The first basketball game in McKale Center (February 1, 1973)-Special Collections, University of Arizona Libraries, University of Arizona Photograph Collection, McKale Memorial Center.

PAGES 19–20

Coach Snowden 1972 hiring press release, courtesy of Arizona Athletic Department: Greg Byrne, Athletic Director; James Francis, Assistant Athletic Director; Cory Walton, Athletics Communications.

PAGES 21–24

Fred Snowden March 1972 resume, courtesy of Arizona Athletic Department: Greg Byrne, Athletic Director; James Francis, Assistant Athletic Director; Cory Walton, Athletics Communications.

PAGE 28

1972–1973 team picture courtesy of George Kalil, from the personal collection of George Kalil.

PAGE 31

Coach Fred Snowden and Assistant Coach Jerry Holmes, 1973, courtesy of Arizona Athletic Department: Greg Byrne, Athletic Director; James Francis, Assistant Athletic Director; Cory Walton, Athletics Communications.

PAGE 37

Eric Money playing against Arizona State (1973), courtesy of Arizona Athletic Department: Greg Byrne, Athletic Director; James Francis, Assistant Athletic Director; Cory Walton, Athletics Communications.

PAGE 38

Coniel Norman playing against Arizona State (1973), courtesy of Arizona Athletic Department: Greg Byrne, Athletic Director; James Francis, Assistant Athletic Director; Cory Walton, Athletics Communications.

PAGE 41

Coach Fred Snowden in action (1973), courtesy of Arizona Athletic Department: Greg Byrne, Athletic Director; James Francis, Assistant Athletic Director; Cory Walton, Athletics Communications.

PAGE 44

Coach Fred Snowden and Arizona Sports Information Director Frank Soltys (1973), courtesy of Arizona Athletic Department: Greg Byrne, Athletic Director; James Francis, Assistant Athletic Director; Cory Walton, Athletics Communications.

PAGE 47

March 1973 picture of Eric Money, bus driver (unnamed), and George Kalil at the University of Wyoming, picture courtesy of George Kalil, from the personal collection of George Kalil.

PAGE 56

1973–1974 team picture courtesy of George Kalil, from the personal collection of George Kalil.

PAGE 62

1973–1974 coaching staff: Assistant Coach Ken Maxey, Assistant Coach Jerry Holmes, Head Coach Fred Snowden, courtesy of Arizona Athletic Department: Greg Byrne, Athletic Director; James Francis, Assistant Athletic Director; Cory Walton, Athletics Communications.

PAGE 64

Arizona versus Illinois, November 30, 1973, official basketball box score, courtesy of Bob Elliott, from the personal collection of Bob Elliott.

PAGE 71

Arizona versus Arizona State, February 2, 1974, Bob Elliott posting up Ron "The Rock" Kennedy of ASU, courtesy of Bob Elliott, from the personal collection of Bob Elliott.

PAGE 75

Coach Fred Snowden in McKale Center (1974), courtesy of Arizona Athletic Department: Greg Byrne, Athletic Director; James Francis, Assistant Athletic Director; Cory Walton, Athletics Communications.

PAGE 77

Arizona versus Texas Tech, December 22, 1973, program, courtesy of Bob Elliott, from the personal collection of Bob Elliott.

PAGE 82

1974–1975 team picture courtesy of George Kalil, from the personal collection of George Kalil.

PAGE 86

Drawing of Wilber the Wildcat by Jackie Baxter Armijo, signed by the 1975 team. Drawing courtesy of Jackie Baxter Armijo and Brian Baxter.

PAGE 90

1975–1976 team picture courtesy of George Kalil, from the personal collection of George Kalil.

PAGE 92

Arizona-Georgetown, March 13, 1976, basketball program courtesy of Bob Elliott, from the personal collection of Bob Elliott.

PAGE 95

Bob Elliott, 1976 free throw against UNLV, courtesy of Bob Elliott, from the personal collection of Bob Elliott.

PAGE 96

Al Fleming and Coach Fred Snowden (1973), courtesy of Arizona Athletic Department: Greg Byrne, Athletic Director; James Francis, Assistant Athletic Director; Cory Walton, Athletics Communications.

PAGE 100

1976–1977 team picture courtesy of George Kalil, from the personal collection of George Kalil.

PAGE 103

Arizona versus Moscow Red Army, basketball program and game ticket, March 6, 1977, courtesy of Bob Elliott, from the personal collection of Bob Elliott.

PAGE 105

1977 Arizona basketball banquet program, courtesy of Bob Elliott, from the personal collection of Bob Elliott.

PAGE 114

Head Coach Fred Snowden and Assistant Coach Len Gordy (1979), courtesy of Arizona Athletic Department: Greg Byrne, Athletic Director; James Francis, Assistant Athletic Director; Cory Walton, Athletics Communications.

PAGE 116

Pac-10 game (1981), Robbie Dosty, Assistant Coach Len Gordy, Assistant Coach Mike Frink, Head Coach Fred Snowden, courtesy of Arizona Athletic Department: Greg Byrne, Athletic Director; James Francis, Assistant Athletic Director; Cory Walton, Athletics Communications.

PAGE 118

Fred Snowden March 1982 letter of resignation, courtesy of Arizona Athletic Department: Greg Byrne, Athletic Director; James Francis, Assistant Athletic Director; Cory Walton, Athletics Communications.

PAGE 120

Fred Snowden memorial service program, January 22, 1994, courtesy of Arizona Athletic Department: Greg Byrne, Athletic Director; James Francis, Assistant Athletic Director; Cory Walton, Athletics Communications.

ARIZONA BASKETBALL RECORDS AND OTHER HIGHLIGHTS, BY YEAR

1946

First Arizona team to play in a postseason tournament game (NIT)

1948

Morris Udall and Linc Richmond, first Arizona players to be drafted in the professional draft

1949

Link Richmond, career scoring, 1,246

1951

Leo Johnson, rebounds, season, 373

Leo Johnson, rebound average, season, 12

Roger Johnson, first All-American to play at Arizona

1956

Bill Reeves, rebounds, game, 26

Bill Reeves, rebound average, season, 13.2

1957

Bill Reeves, rebounds, career, 837

1960

Ernie McCray, points scored, game, 46

Ernie McCray, points scored, career, 1,349

1962

Joe Skaisgir, rebounds, game, 26

Joe Skaisgir, scoring average, career, 19.9

Joe Skaisgir, rebound average, career, 11.2

1965

Warren Rustand, first Academic All-American to play at Arizona

1971

Bill Warner, points scored, career, 1,462

1972

Coniel Norman, points per game, career, 23.9

Coniel Norman, scoring average, season, 24.0

1974

Al Fleming, field goal percentage, season, .667

1975

Al Fleming, field goal percentage, game (min. 10 attempts) 10 of 10, 1.000

Bob Elliott, field goals, season, 273

First Arizona team ranked in the top ten

1976

Al Fleming, rebounds, career, 1,190

Al Fleming, points scored, career, 1,765

First Arizona team to play in the NCAA tournament Elite Eight

1977

Bob Elliott, points scored, career, 2,125

Bob Elliott, free throws, career, 515

First Arizona team to play in consecutive NCAA tournaments

1979

Russell Brown, assists, game, 19

Russell Brown, assists, season, 247

Larry Demic, first Arizona player drafted in the first round of the NBA draft

1980

Joe Nehls, free throw percentage, career, .855

1981

Russell Brown, assists, career, 810

1983

Pete Williams, field goal percentage, career, .605 (296 of 489)

1988

Steve Kerr, three-point field goal percentage, season, .573

Steve Kerr, three-point field goal percentage, career, .573

Steve Kerr, three-point field goals, season, 114

Steve Kerr, free throw percentage, season, .899

First Arizona team to play at the NCAA Final Four

1989

Sean Elliott, free throws made, career, 623

Anthony Cook, blocked shots season, 84

Anthony Cook, blocked shots, career, 278

Sean Elliott, career scoring, 2555

1990

Matt Muehlebach, first triple-double by an Arizona
player (10 points, 11 rebounds, 10 assists)

Matt Othick, three-point field goals, career, 191

1994

Dylan Rigdon, free throw percentage, career, .872

Second Arizona team to play in the NCAA Final
Four

1993

Khalid Reeves, points scored, season, 848

1995

Damon Stoudamire, three-point field goals, career,
272

Bob Elliott, first and only Arizona student-athlete
inducted into the Academic All-American Hall
of Fame

1996

Joseph Blair, field goal percentage, season, .690 (89 of 129 in 14 games)

1997

Jason Terry, steals, season, 85

First NCAA basketball national championship

Third Arizona team to reach the NCAA Final Four

1998

Bennett Davison, steals, game, 9

Mike Bibby, steals, season, 87

1999

Jason Terry, steals, career, 245

2000

Loren Woods, blocked shots, game, 14

Loren Woods, blocked shots, season, 102

2001

Fourth Arizona team to reach the NCAA Final Four

NCAA Final Four runner-up

2002

Coach Lute Olson inducted into the Naismith Memorial Basketball Hall of Fame

2005

Salim Stoudamire, three-point field goals, game, 9

Salim Stoudamire, three-point field goals, season, 120

Salim Stoudamire, three-point field goals, career, 342

Salim Stoudamire, free throw percentage, season, .910

2006
Jawaan McClellan, three-point field goal percentage, game, 1.000 (7 of 7)

2008
Jerryd Bayless, free throws made, game, 18

2009
Jordan Hill, rebounds, season, 375

2011
Derrick Williams, free throws made, season, 247

RETIRED JERSEYS
Sean Elliott 1985–1989, jersey retired in 1996
Steve Kerr 1983–1988, jersey retired in 1999
Mike Bibby 1996–1998, jersey retired in 2004
Jason Gardner 1999–2003, jersey retired in 2005

ARIZONA YEARLY RESULTS

YEAR	COACH	WINS	LOSSES	ATTENDANCE
1904–05	Orin Kates	1	0	
1905–06	Orin Kates	(Intrasquad Games Only)		
1906–07	Unknown	3	1	
1907–08	Unknown	1	2	
1908–09	Unknown	1	1	
1909–10	Unknown	2	2	
1910–11	Unknown	3	0	
1911–12	Frank Kleeberger	2	2	
1912–13	Raymond Quigley	3	2	
1913–14	Raymond Quigley	7	2	
1914–15	J. F. McKale	9	0	
1915–16	J. F. McKale	5	0	
1916–17	J. F. McKale	10	2	
1917–18	J. F. McKale	3	2	
1918–19	J. F. McKale	6	3	
1919–20	J. F. McKale	9	5	
1920–21	J. F. McKale	7	0	
1921–22	James Pierce	10	2	
1922–23	James Pierce	17	3	
1923–24	Basil Stanley	14	3	
1924–25	Walter Davis	7	4	
1925–26	Fred A. Enke	6	7	
1926–27	Fred A. Enke	13	4	
1927–28	Fred A. Enke	13	3	
1928–29	Fred A. Enke	19	4	

YEAR	COACH	WINS	LOSSES	ATTENDANCE
1929–30	Fred A. Enke	15	6	
1930–31	Fred A. Enke	9	6	
1931–32	Fred A. Enke	18	2	
1932–33	Fred A. Enke	19	5	
1933–34	Fred A. Enke	18	9	
1934–35	Fred A. Enke	11	8	
1935–36	Fred A. Enke	16	7	
1936–37	Fred A. Enke	14	11	
1937–38	Fred A. Enke	13	8	
1938–39	Fred A. Enke	12	11	
1939–40	Fred A. Enke	15	10	
1940–41	Fred A. Enke	11	7	
1941–42	Fred A. Enke	9	13	
1942–43	Fred A. Enke	22	2	
1943–44	Fred A. Enke	12	2	
1944–45	Fred A. Enke	7	11	
1945–46	Fred A. Enke	25	5	
1946–47	Fred A. Enke	21	3	
1947–48	Fred A. Enke	19	10	
1948–49	Fred A. Enke	17	11	
1949–50	Fred A. Enke	26	5	
1950–51	Fred A. Enke	24	6	
1951–52	Fred A. Enke	11	16	
1952–53	Fred A. Enke	13	11	
1953–54	Fred A. Enke	14	10	
1954–55	Fred A. Enke	8	17	
1955–56	Fred A. Enke	11	15	
1956–57	Fred A. Enke	13	13	
1957–58	Fred A. Enke	10	15	

YEAR	COACH	WINS	LOSSES	ATTENDANCE
1958–59	Fred A. Enke	4	22	
1959–60	Fred A. Enke	10	14	
1960–61	Fred A. Enke	11	15	
1961–62	Bruce Larson	12	14	
1962–63	Bruce Larson	13	13	
1963–64	Bruce Larson	15	11	
1964–65	Bruce Larson	17	9	
1965–66	Bruce Larson	15	11	
1966–67	Bruce Larson	8	17	
1967–68	Bruce Larson	11	13	
1968–69	Bruce Larson	17	10	
1969–70	Bruce Larson	12	14	
1970–71	Bruce Larson	10	16	
1971–72	Bruce Larson	6	20	
1972–73	Fred Snowden	16	10	12,995
1973–74	Fred Snowden	19	7	12,285
1974–75	Fred Snowden	22	7	11,364
1975–76	Fred Snowden	24	9	11,220
1976–77	Fred Snowden	21	6	12,446
1977–78	Fred Snowden	15	11	11,495
1978–79	Fred Snowden	16	11	11,655
1979–80	Fred Snowden	12	15	11,339
1980–81	Fred Snowden	13	14	9,450
1981–82	Fred Snowden	9	18	8,234
1982–83	Ben Lindsey	4	24	6,224
1983–84	Lute Olson	11	17	7,297
1984–85	Lute Olson	21	10	10,932
1985–86	Lute Olson	23	9	11,188
1986–87	Lute Olson	18	12	12,720

YEAR	COACH	WINS	LOSSES	ATTENDANCE
1987–88	Lute Olson	35	3	13,297
1988–89	Lute Olson	29	4	13,620
1989–90	Lute Olson	25	7	13,639
1990–91	Lute Olson	28	7	13,826
1991–92	Lute Olson	24	7	13,884
1992–93	Lute Olson	24	4	13,879
1993–94	Lute Olson	29	6	13,973
1994–95	Lute Olson	24	7	14,257
1995–96	Lute Olson	27	6	14,254
1996–97	Lute Olson	25	9	14,279
1997–98	Lute Olson	30	5	14,530
1998–99	Lute Olson	22	6	14,349
	(actual)	22	7	
1999–2000	Lute Olson	27	7	14,485
2000–01	Lute Olson/			
	Jim Rosborough	28	8	14,533
2001–02	Lute Olson	24	10	14,544
2002–03	Lute Olson	28	4	14,562
2003–04	Lute Olson	20	10	14,561
2004–05	Lute Olson	30	7	14,558
2005–06	Lute Olson	20	13	14,587
2006–07	Lute Olson	20	11	14,202
2007–08	Kevin O'Neill	0	14	14,218
	(actual)	19	15	
2008–09	Russ Pennell	21	14	13,681
2009–10	Sean Miller	16	15	13,815
2010–11	Sean Miller	30	8	13,680
2011–12	Sean Miller	23	12	13,602
2012–13	Sean Miller	27	8	14,157

YEAR	SCORING	REBOUNDING	ASSISTS
1904–1920	No stats recorded		
1920–21	A. L. Slonaker		
1921–22	A. L. Slonaker		
1922–23	Harold Tovrea		
1923–24	Harold Tovrea		
1924–25	Clarence Skousen		
1925–26	Byron Drachman		
1926–27	Charles Miller		
1927–28	Larry Edwards		
1928–29	Neal Goodman		
1929–30	Neal Goodman		
1930–31	Jack Raffety		
1931–32	Howard Abbott		
1932–33	Jack Raffety		
1933–34	Vince Byrne		
1934–35	Walt Scoltzhauer		
1935–36	Lorry DiGrazia		
1936–37	Lorry DiGrazia		
1937–38	Lorry DiGrazia		
1938–39	George Jordan		
1939–40	George Jordan		
1940–41	Vince Cullen		
1941–42	Vince Cullen		
1942–43	Bob Ruman		
1943–44	George Genung		
1944–45	Jimmy Steele		
1945–46	Link Richmond		
1946–47	Link Richmond		
1947–48	Morris Udall		

YEAR	SCORING	REBOUNDING	ASSISTS
1948–49	Leon Blevins		
1949–50	Leon Blevins		
1950–51	Bob Honea	Leo Johnson	Leo Johnson
1951–52	Bill Kemmeries	Jerry Dillon	Roger Johnson
1952–53	Bill Kemmeries	Teddy Lazovich	
1953–54	Hadie Redd	Hadie Redd	
1954–55	Hadie Redd	Hadie Redd	
1955–56	Ed Nymeyer	Bill Reeves	
1956–57	Ed Nymeyer	Bill Reeves	
1957–58	Ed Nymeyer	Ernie McCray	
1958–59	Ernie McCray	Ernie McCray	
1959–60	Ernie McCray	Ernie McCray	
1960–61	Joe Skaisgir	Joe Skaisgir	
1961–62	Joe Skaisgir	Joe Skaisgir	
1962–63	Albert Johnson	Albert Johnson	
1963–64	Albert Johnson	Albert Johnson	
1964–65	Warren Rustand	Albert Johnson	
1965–66	Ted Pickett	Mike Aboud	
1966–67	Bill Davis	Bill Davis	
1967–68	Bill Davis	Bill Davis	
1968–69	Bill Warner	Eddie Myers	
1969–70	Bill Warner	Tom Lee	
1970–71	Bill Warner	Eddie Myers	
1971–72	Jim Huckestein	Lynard Harris	
1972–73	Coniel Norman	Al Fleming	Eric Money
1973–74	Coniel Norman	Bob Elliott	Eric Money
1974–75	Bob Elliott	Al Fleming	Gilbert Myles
1975–76	Bob Elliott	Bob Elliott	Jim Rappis
1976–77	Herman Harris	Phil Taylor	Gary Harrison

TUCSON A BASKETBALL TOWN

YEAR	SCORING	REBOUNDING	ASSISTS
1977–78	Phil Taylor	Phil Taylor	Russell Brown
1978–79	Larry Demic	Larry Demic	Russell Brown
1979–80	Joe Nehls	Frank Smith	Russell Brown
1980–81	Ron Davis	Robbie Dosty	Russell Brown
1981–82	Greg Cook	Frank Smith	Ricky Walker
1982–83	Frank Smith	Frank Smith	Brock Brunkhorst
1983–84	Pete Williams	Pete Williams	Brock Brunkhorst
1984–85	Eddie Smith	Pete Williams	Brock Brunkhorst
1985–86	Sean Elliott	John Edgar	Steve Kerr
1986–87	Sean Elliott	Anthony Cook	Sean Elliott
1987–88	Sean Elliott	Anthony Cook	Steve Kerr
1988–89	Sean Elliott	Anthony Cook	Ken Lofton
1989–90	Jud Buechler	Jud Buechler	Matt Muehlebach
1990–91	Chris Mills	Brian Williams	Matt Othick
1991–92	Sean Rooks	Chris Mills	Matt Othick
1992–93	Chris Mills	Chris Mills	Damon Stoudamire
1993–94	Khalid Reeves	Ray Owes	Damon Stoudamire
1994–95	Damon Stoudamire	Ray Owes	Damon Stoudamire
1995–96	Ben Davis	Ben Davis	Reggie Geary
1996–97	Michael Dickerson	A. J. Bramlett	Mike Bibby
1997–98	Michael Dickerson	A. J. Bramlett	Mike Bibby
1998–99	Jason Terry	A. J. Bramlett	Jason Terry
1999–2000	Loren Woods	Michael Wright	Jason Gardner
2000–01	Gilbert Arenas	Michael Wright	Jason Gardner
2001–02	Jason Gardner	Luke Walton	Luke Walton
2002–03	Jason Gardner	Channing Frye	Jason Gardner
2003–04	Hassan Adams	Andre Iguodala	Andre Iguodala
2004–05	Salim Stoudamire	Channing Frye	Mustafa Shakur

ARIZONA YEARLY RESULTS

YEAR	SCORING	REBOUNDING	ASSISTS
2005–06	Hassan Adams	Ivan Radenovic	Mustafa Shakur
2006–07	Marcus Williams	Ivan Radenovic	Mustafa Shakur
2007–08	Jerryd Bayless	Jordan Hill	Jerryd Bayless
2008–09	Chase Budinger	Jordan Hill	Nic Wise
2009–10	Derrick Williams	Derrick Williams	Nic Wise
2010–11	Derrick Williams	Derrick Williams	Kyle Fogg
2011–12	Kyle Fogg	Solomon Hill	Solomon Hill
2012–13	Mark Lyons	Kaleb Tarczewski	Nick Johnson

ABOUT THE AUTHORS

Robert A. Elliott is founder and president of Elliott Accounting, an accounting, tax, management, and investment advisory services firm. Bob is currently the lead director for UNS Energy and has served as the chairman of the Board of the NBA Retired Players Association, Tucson Airport Authority, Tucson Metropolitan Chamber of Commerce, University of Arizona Alumni Association, and Tucson Urban League. He is currently serving as a board member of AAA of Arizona, the NBA Retired Players Association, the University of Arizona Foundation, and the University of Arizona Eller College of Business. Mr. Elliott is a member of Sigma Pi Phi fraternity and is a NAACP life member.

Mr. Elliott enjoyed a twenty-seven-year television and radio broadcasting analyst career. He has voice credits with EA Sports for NBA Live 2003, 2002, and 2001, as well as NBA Street. He played professional basketball for the New Jersey Nets for three years. Mr. Elliott was a three time college basketball Athletic and Academic All-American, and he is the only University of Arizona athlete to be a member of the College Academic All-American Hall of Fame.

Eric Money was drafted in the second round by the Detroit Pistons and enjoyed a six-year career in the NBA with the Detroit Pistons, New Jersey Nets, and Philadelphia 76ers. He averaged 12.2 points per game in his NBA career. Money was also one of the many professional basketball players to appear in the 1979 film *The Fish That Saved Pittsburgh* starring Julius "Dr. J" Erving. He is currently coaching and providing individualized player development for kids.